Life's Unexpected Blessings

Life's Unexpected Blessings

MS. MICHELLE COPELAND

Kravitz & Sons
INNOVATORS IN PUBLISHING, MARKETING AND ADVERTISING

Kravitz and Sons LLC
1301 Farmville Blvd, Suite 104
Greenville, NC 27834

© 2025 Michelle Copeland. All rights reserved.

No part of this book may be reproduced, stored in a retrieval system, or transmitted by any means without the written permission of the author.

Published by Kravitz and Sons LLC.

ISBN:	979-8-89639-303-0 (sc)
ISBN:	979-8-89639-302-3 (e)
ISBN:	979-8-89639-326-9 (h)

Library of Congress Control Number: 2025909398

Because of the dynamic nature of the Internet, any web addresses or links contained in this book may have changed since publication and may no longer be valid. The views expressed in this work are solely those of the author and do not necessarily reflect the views of the publisher, and the publisher hereby disclaims any responsibility for them.

Table of Contents

Chapter 1 1

Chapter 2 3

Chapter 3 7

Chapter 4 11

Chapter 5 13

Chapter 6 17

Chapter 7 19

Chapter 8 23

Chapter 9 27

Chapter 10 31

Chapter 11 35

Chapter 12 37

Chapter 13 41

Chapter 14 45

Chapter 15 53

Chapter 16 57

Chapter 17 61

Chapter 18 65

Chapter 19 71

Chapter 1

Have you ever been asked the question where do you see yourself in ten years? Sheila saw herself married to a good, honest man with whom she had two children. She also saw herself with a good job where she made a difference and that she enjoyed like a doctor. Instead she is a single, thirty-five-year-old woman with no children living with her mom and older sister. And she can also add jobless to the list. "Sheila! Earth to Sheila. Are you here?" Her mom is standing over the kitchen sink washing dishes.

"Yes, ma'am."

"What are you thinking about now?"

"Nothing." She's standing over the stove frying chicken.

"You are thinking about something. And if you don't tell me I'll tickle it out of you." Her mom gets closer and closer. Then her fingers pounce under her arms, and she lets out a big giggle. Sheila surrenders. "Okay! Okay!" Sheila's mom does not like to see her baby sad or crying. "I'm just thinking about my life." Her mom gets this puzzled look on her face.

"What about your life?"

"It would be nice to earn some money of my own and no one will hire me or give me the opportunity to prove myself. And you need help taking care of Linda and things around the house. I can't see myself holding down a regular nine to five job and excelling at it."

"So what has your brilliant mind came up with?" her mom says sweetly but joking at the same time.

"Well, people seem to like my art. Maybe I could put on an art show and see if I can sell some of my art work." Her mom pauses for a few moments.

"That is an idea."

"What does that mean?"

"Well, have you really thought this through? The money, the location, the food, etc.?"

"I'm still working the details out in my mind."

"Okay. Well, one thing I know for sure is when you set your mind to something and are determined you can do anything. And most of the time you accomplish what you set out to do. Let's eat! I'm hungry."

A voice from the family room rings out, "Is dinner ready?"

Sheila yells back, "Yes, I'm fixing your plate right now." She puts a fried drumstick, a spoonful of mac and cheese, and green beans on a plate. She walks briskly with the plate in one hand into the family room and hands it to her sister.

She responds rudely, "I want some Tabasco sauce."

"You have two good legs that work so if you want some Tabasco sauce I suggest you get it yourself."

"Okay, you're right." Linda reluctantly gets up and proceeds to the kitchen to retrieve the Tabasco sauce. After dinner Sheila retires to her room. As she watches Family Feud several thoughts run through her head. Sheila is thinking hopefully she'll get an hour or two to herself before her name is called. She loves her sister, but she acts like a baby. Her sister has health problems, but she's not helpless. Sheila wishes her sister was more motivated to be independent. Most people mistake Sheila for the older sister, but she's the younger sister. Well, that's her sister whom she loves. Sheila tries to focus on the blessings in her life. She is blessed to have a roof over her head, food to eat, clothes on her back, a few good friends, and a family that loves her. She is grateful and thankful for all those things. She might not have her dad here anymore, but she knows he is here in spirit while watching over her in heaven. And she still has her mom and sister. Right now her mom needs her help to care for her sister especially when it comes to the medical stuff at this moment in time. She had a plan for herself, but God has other plans for her—she believes better and greater plans. She puts her faith in God. That is what her family has always done and will continue to do. He has never forsaken her or her family even when she thought he had. When she is weak He is strong. And through Him all things are possible.

As she lies there in bed and falls off to sleep she hears a soft, kind voice whisper, "Always remember this."

Chapter 2

The light from the sun shines through her bedroom window waking Sheila from a peaceful, yet restless sleep. She forces herself to get out of the bed to face another day that could bring frustration, aggravation, tears, sorrow, laughter, joy, or all of the above. As she comes out of her room Sheila hears Linda's voice. "Do we have any sausage?"

"I think we have sage sausage. Do you want a fried egg and toast with it?" She hesitates a moment.

"Okay" Their mom appears in the doorway still asleep, staggering. Sheila lets out a giggle. Their mom is still not quite awake yet.

"It's not funny. What do you need help with?"

"Well, you can empty Linda's ostomy bag while I start breakfast and get her medications together."

"Okay, honey!"

"Thanks, Mom!" After Sheila makes her a cup of coffee she wakes up a little. Her mom and Sheila are a good, strong team. Her mom always says Sheila does the cooking and she does the cleaning up. After breakfast and once Sheila has taken care of her sister and reminded her mom of what she needs to do, she goes outside to do some needed yard work. Working in the yard/garden is relaxing for Sheila and helps her think when it is quiet. It's meditation for Sheila. She feels like she's close to God having a conversation. God speaks in a quiet, still voice, not in a boisterous, booming voice. After finishing up cleaning and straightening the kitchen, her mom soon comes outside to join the fun with a big grin on her face.

"What are you up to out here?"

"Nothing! I was going to plant these flowers you bought yesterday. Do you like where I placed them?"

"I like them there. They look beautiful there and they brighten up this area nicely. They give it some color. You know something? You have a knack for gardening." Her mom gives Sheila a big hug.

Sheila responds while hugging her back, "I get it from you." Then Sheila gives her a little tickle under her arms and her mom begins laughing.

"You're sneaky and if anybody saw us they would think we're crazy." Then Sheila begins laughing and a big smile comes across her face.

"I am and you are too!" Then they plant the flowers together and then Sheila helps her trim some shrubs. Sheila's mom loves flowers. Her yard is full of flowers and shrubs of different colors and varieties in the front and back. Just about everyone compliments her mom on the yard and how pretty it is. Cars slow down to a stop almost to get a good look or they're just being nosey. Sheila always thought that was strange because she lives here. She remembers her mom telling her stories about her grandma's garden being big, beautiful, and full of flowers and bright green shrubs mostly. Her grandma also had fruit trees and a vegetable garden. That is from where Sheila's mom got her love of flowers.

All of a sudden, Sheila hears a voice that sounds very close say, "Hi, Evelynn! Hi, Sheila!" She looks up and it's their neighbor Mrs. Ladune taking her trash to the side of the road. She always takes her trash to the side of the road early. Mrs. Ladune and her husband are very friendly and good neighbors. They can be quite funny at times. They can make Sheila and her mom smile. If Sheila needs help with fixing something, her husband always helps her. He has never really said no to her. Sheila's glad God put them next door. Now her other neighbors, not so much. That's a different story. They're weird, crazy, loud, and keep you up half of the night or all night and drink a lot. The yard is trashy with stuff sprawled all across their lawn sometimes. Sheila's other neighbor next door really enjoys setting off fireworks— the louder and bigger the better. They don't care if it's not a holiday. They'll set fireworks off anytime of the day or night, but their mom doesn't like them. The lights they put on are pretty, but the noise hurts Sheila's and her mom's ears. They make a big mess that Sheila and her mom find in their yard sometimes.

As Mrs. Ladune is going back into her house her mom says, "Oh, hi Cynthia!" Then Sheila waves and smiles back at her. God has His reasons for things and most of the time He knows what he is doing. Sheila doesn't understand them, but we're not meant to until He chooses to reveal them.

Life's a mystery to which only God knows the answer. Once again you must have faith. "I think it's time to quit and start dinner."

"I think you're right, Mom. And we need to check on Linda too." Mom agrees as they walk into the kitchen.

"I'll check on Linda and you start dinner." In the middle of cooking Sheila remembers that it's medication time for her sister. She stops to give it to her while her mom takes over cooking duty. Sheila returns to her cooking while her mom is cleaning up the kitchen as they go. That night her mind goes back to the art showcase. She's thinking maybe she can rent a banquet room at a hotel and forgo catering. But what if no one shows up? What if it costs too much to rent a space? She thinks maybe she should consider entering an art festival. All she would have to pay is an entry or booth fee. But what if no one likes or buys her art?

She hears that soft, kind voice whisper, "Take a risk and have faith in me and trust me."

Chapter 3

As morning dawns Sheila wakes up to the same old grind or routine. Her mom tells her the faucet is leaking in the tub. "Okay. When I get the chance I'll call the plumber." Sheila gets her sister settled and proceeds to pay some bills online for her mom. After that she makes an appointment for Carlos to come out and fix the leaky faucet. After that Sheila sees what her mom needs help with and makes sure she didn't forget to take her medication. As they eat lunch Sheila mentions that Carlos will be out to the house in a few days to fix the leaky faucet. She reminds her of Linda's appointment with one of her doctors tomorrow. Sheila also reminds her mom that she has an appointment with her doctor next week. "Hey, Mom! Do you remember when I mentioned putting on an art show?"

"Yes, I think so. But I don't have the money to give you to put one on. If I did I would give it to you."

"I know, Mom. But I was thinking about entering an art festival. I would only have to pay a small fee and the food and beverages would be taken care of. I know people will be there. Now if they are going to buy any of my artwork I don't know. There's an art festival in about two months in the park downtown. And they're giving out cash prizes to the best pieces of art."

"Well, that doesn't sound bad. When did you work this out?"

"When I was paying bills online I did some research on art festivals." Her mom looks at Sheila strangely with amazement.

"I have a very smart, determined daughter. She's also a good, kind person who thinks about others especially her family. Your dad would be very proud of you. If you want to you can enter the art festival, and I'll pay the fee."

"Thank you, Mamma! You're the best and I love you very much. I hope you're right about dad being proud of me and I miss him."

"We all miss him. And I know your dad is proud of you." The next day Mom and Sheila take Linda to her doctor's appointment. At one time Sheila seriously thought about becoming a doctor. She even went to college and studied medicine. She applied to medical school but she didn't get in. Before she could apply again her dad became sick. Sheila put things aside and focused on helping her mom care for him till the end. He was sick for six or seven years, but it felt longer to her. It was hard to see this strong and proud man, her father, over time gradually turn into a frail and sick old man who didn't know Mom, Linda, or her from Adam and Eve. But Sheila chooses to hold onto the good memories. Sheila's mom needed her and her support. Because of the little knowledge of medicine she learned in school and the courses she took in college she was better able to understand his doctors, follow their instructions, and then interpret for her family. Sheila always wanted to help people, but now her sister's doctors have changed her mind. She doesn't think she fits into today's medical field. She's not particularly fond of Linda's doctors. She dreads taking her sister to her appointments. Her doctors don't accept this particular insurance or they refuse to deal with Medicaid and prefer to deal with Medicare. They refer her to this doctor and that doctor refers her to another doctor. They can't do this or that. If you do this and talk to this person this should happen and it doesn't. It never ends. Sometimes they're just rude, arrogant, and don't listen to Sheila or take into account anything her mom, Linda, or she has to say. They have the opinion that they're the doctors so they're right, and people should just shut up and do what they say. Sheila doesn't always agree with the way they choose to treat her sister's condition or that she honestly needs all these meds they put her on. The only one who is always right and knows best is God. The last time she checked doctors aren't God. They're human. They are instruments of God through which he guides and helps them to heal, care for, and help others. Sheila thought medicine was about treating and helping the sick/ill in need, not about making sure you get paid first. The person/patient should always come first and the money last. But Linda's doctors feel the opposite way. Her appointment went pretty well. But he was very rude and refused to understand or take into account anything Linda's mom or Sheila was saying. Yet he wanted Sheila and her mom to listen to him and understand what he was saying while getting a little frustrated and annoyed at the same time with them. At least this time Sheila wasn't in tears like she usually is. She gets so frustrated. The next day Sheila finds some time somewhere to fill out paper work for the art festival and write the check for the entry fee. As she puts it in the mailbox she sees the plumber pull up in the driveway. He gets out the car and begins walking towards Sheila.

"Hi, Carlos!"

"Hey, how's it going?" "Good. And how about you?"

"The same. I have no complaints."

"That's good to hear." Carlos and Sheila walk through the kitchen door to find her mom standing over the sink.

"Hey, Carlos! How are things going with you and how's the family?"

"I'm good and so is the family."

"How are those beautiful children of yours?" Carlos gets this big grin across his face.

"They're getting bigger and they're something else." Then he lets out a big laugh. Then Sheila and her mom start smiling as he shows them pictures of the children. After they finish gushing over his children, Sheila shows him the problem. Carlos follows Sheila to the bathroom where she shows him the leaky tub faucet. "It's an easy fix. All you need is a new part. This one is old and corroded. It should cost your mom around $200$250."

"Okay. That sounds good." As they're chatting while he's working Sheila notices he has a really nice, warm smile. "So, what's been up with you?"

"Uh, me! Nothing much. My sister's health has not been good. She's been in and out of the hospital for the last year or so."

"I'm sorry to hear that."

"Well I got divorced about two years ago."

Sheila is moderately shocked and surprised. "I'm sorry to hear that. How are you really doing?"

"Don't be sorry because I'm not. It's the best thing that ever happened to me. I'm happier, she's happier, and the children are happier." As Carlos finishes up Sheila writes out the check. Then a few moments later she hears his voice. "Okay. I'm done. That should do it." As Sheila hands him the check she thanks him. He takes the check from her hand. "All I need is a signature right here from you or your mom." She hears her mom's voice coming out of the kitchen.

"Sheila can sign for me." So Sheila signs the paper and walks Carlos to the door.

Chapter 4

Sheila's mind goes back to the art festival. Will anyone buy her artwork or even like it? As the date of the art festival approaches Sheila becomes more nervous. Sheila thinks to herself at least she has enough stuff to keep her preoccupied. She goes down the list in her head mentally. She needs to call in medicine for her mom and Linda. She also needs to call Linda's medical insurance and make an appointment for her mom to see her doctor. Something else she just remembers. She needs to call the cable company. When Sheila and her mom were outside doing some yard work she cut the cable line unknowingly. They were transplanting a bush from the backyard to the front. One day this week or next the yard needs cutting and edging. Sheila needs to fix the kitchen chairs too. The spokes or legs of the chairs are coming out or apart so she needs to glue those back in. It's always never ending—one thing after another that needs to be taken care of. At least it keeps her busy and out of trouble, and her time and energy is spent in a more constructive manner. This morning she wakes up with the plan in her mind to cut the front yard at least and maybe do the back tomorrow. Sheila has learned over time that sometimes you can't plan for things and you just have to go with the flow. But you can try your hardest to be prepared for things. Of course she makes sure Linda's taken care of first and Mom did the stuff she needed to do for herself. It's such a nice, cool day that Sheila decides to go outside and start cutting the front yard. Soon after that her mom joins her outside. After an hour or two of being at work, Mom and Sheila take a break. She goes in the house to check on Linda and to get some water for her and her mom. It's also time for Linda to take some more medication. After checking on Linda and taking a water break, Sheila goes back outside and notices her mom talking to Mrs. Brooks. Today she has her dog, Spunky, and three children she's babysitting. As Sheila approaches the two of them Mrs. Brooks says, "Hi, Sheila!"

She hands the glass of water to her mom. "Hi, Mrs. Brooks!" While the two of them are chatting she plays with Spunky and the children. They're talking, laughing, and having fun. The children like to look at the flowers in the yard. Sheila feels a hand on her shoulder. She looks up and it's her mom.

"They have to go now."

"Okay. Bye!" And they all wave back goodbye. After Sheila and her mom finish up in the yard they head inside to start dinner. As they're cooking Sheila's thinking about the approaching art festival. She needs to choose what artwork she's showing. A few days later Sheila finds the time to look at her artwork and decides which paintings or sketches to show. Her sister is telling her which ones she likes. They hear their mom yelling as she walks through the front door.

"I'm back! Where's everybody?" Then she hears Sheila yelling back from her bedroom. She heads in that direction and stops at the door. "What's going on in here?"

"I'm trying to figure out which pieces of art to show at the festival and Linda is helping sort of," Linda chimes in abruptly.

"Is everything okay? What did the doctor say?"

"I'm fine. The doctor says I'm doing well and I'm scheduled to go back to do blood work in a couple of months."

"Mom which one of these do you like?"

"I like them all, honey. They're all beautiful. But I wouldn't mind keeping this one and that one too. And I especially love these two."

"Well, that helps me narrow it down. I washed a load of clothes, straightened up the family room, and cleaned the bathrooms."

"Thank you, sweetie. I picked up the medicine you called in for me and Linda."

Chapter 5

The day of the art festival has arrived, and Sheila's mom helps her load up the car. "I wish I was going with you, but someone has to stay with Linda."

"I know. I wrote down instructions for Linda. What medications to give her at what times and so on. If there is an emergency or you need something call me on my cell. Linda is pretty much taken care of and I should be home by late afternoon. If you want I can pick up some dinner on the way home."

"Don't be nervous and you'll do fine. Please be careful and safe. If you feel up to it you can pick up some food."

"Okay, Mom. See you later." When Sheila arrives at the festival she sets her booth up fairly quickly with no problems. As she looks around at the other booths she sees some beautiful artwork. The young lady in the booth next to her compliments her artwork. She thinks it's bright, bold, and positive. Hers is interesting and abstract. As the festival is about to open Sheila feels nervous, but more excited than anything. She calls her mom to let her know she arrived safely. Her mom can sense she's a little nervous so she tries to ease her nerves. A few people start to approach her booth and she ends the phone call feeling less nervous. So far she has been meeting some very friendly and interesting people. As the day progresses more and more people approach her booth. They all show interest and compliment her art, but only a few buy pieces of her art. Sheila suddenly sees a familiar face in the crowd looking at her art with his two children. She realizes it's Carlos, but he looks different out of his work clothes. He's kind of cute. Carlos looks up, surprised.

"Hey, Sheila! This is your art?"

She's surprised to see him too. "Yes. And these are your adorable children?"

"Oh, yeah! This is Sophia and Max."

"Hi! I like the butterfly on the flower," Max chimes in. "I like the big bird in the sky."

"They're all beautiful. How have you done so far? It's just you today?"

"Yeah, it's just me. So far a few people bought some of my art. So, what are you guys up to?"

"I have Sophia and Max for the weekend and I thought it would be nice to hang out at the park and enjoy the festival."

Sheila turns to Sophia and Max. "Are you guys having fun with Dad? Did he win you some prizes?"

Sophia is snuggling a stuffed horse close to her chest. "Yes, ma'am. Dad got us some ice cream, popcorn, and hotdogs. He won me this pony too."

Max jumps in, "We rode the bumper cars and the Ferris wheel and the duck boats."

Sophia jumps back in, "We fed the ducks too and some other animals. Can you paint a butterfly on my face?"

"I don't have the right paint for that with me. But next time I will, Sophia. You guys sound like you're having a lot of fun."

"Now we're going to watch a play. Do you want to come too?"

"I would love to, but I should stay in case some more people want to buy my art. Thank you for asking."

"That's our cue to leave. We don't want to miss the play. We'll see you later, Sheila."

"Okay. Bye!" They walk away hand and hand while waving goodbye. "Dad, she seems really nice. I like her. Can we go back after the play to her booth?"

"Yes, if you want to."

"Why don't you ask her to hang out with you next weekend? You won't have me and Max there. The house will be empty and lonely."

"Yeah, Dad!"

"Okay. I'll give it some thought, Sophia and Max. Let's get to this play."

The judges have arrived at Sheila's booth. They are intensely looking at her art. She stands there quietly and nervously trying to read their faces. But she is having no luck reading them. After the judges ask a few questions they move on to the next booth. Soon the winners are announced. Sheila is not hoping for much. If she wins something that's cool and if she doesn't that's cool too. Sheila receives honorable mention and they award her $500. As the festival comes to an end she's tired and happy at the same time. She can't wait to get home and climb into bed. As Sheila starts to pack her booth up she hears a voice. "Would you like some help?" When she turns around she sees that it's Carlos and his children.

"I would love some help. Thank you." As they clean up and pack up the art the children go on about the play. Sophia and Max are very sweet, smart, and observant children. Suddenly.

Sophia bursts out, "I love this one!"

And Max chimes in, "Me too!"

"Well, then you should have it." A big grin comes over the children's faces.

"How much do I owe you, Sheila?" "Nothing. It's a thank you for helping me."

"Thanks! That's very sweet of you." They finish straightening up the booth and start taking boxes to Sheila's car. She can tell Carlos wants to say something, but he seems nervous. Finally Carlos says it. "Do you want to hang out next weekend? I won't have Sophia and Max."

"Okay. Here's my card and give me a call. And thank you for your help, Sophia and Max. I would have still been here."

"You're welcome, Ms. Sheila. Bye!"

Sheila heads home stopping off at KFC to pick up dinner. Before she even walks through the door she hears her sister's voice. "Did you sell any art?"

Then she hears her mom's voice. "I was about to call the sheriff! I was getting a little worried. How was it?"

"I'm fine and it was good. I did sell some art and I won honorable mention, a prize of $500. I also saw Carlos and his children." Sheila's mom gets this funny grin on her face.

"You had an eventful day. How much did you make?" "I made close to $2,000. And Carlos asked me out."

Her mom gets this shocked, surprised look on her face. "Isn't Carlos married?"

"Not anymore. He's been divorced for almost two years. Carlos and his children helped me clean up and load the car."

Now she has a very interested look on her face. "What did you say?" "I said yes. We're going out next weekend." The whole time Linda is watching and listening to every word while sitting at the kitchen table. She's making sure that she doesn't miss any details. They finish the conversation during dinner which includes people she met or saw, Carlos, and the art.

Chapter 6

The next day Sheila's thoughts go to Carlos. A few moments later Sheila hears her name being called. Her mom wants to know how to do these Stouffer's French pizzas. She doesn't want it. Linda's the one who wants it. Sheila goes ahead and makes them for her sister. She figures it's just easier that way. Later that evening she Skypes with her best friend, Eliza, from college. Sheila misses her and wishes she lived closer. They catch up talking about her three children and her husband. Sheila can see them in the background making funny faces and they are cracking her up. Eliza yells at them to quit it. Then they start talking about the art festival. Sheila mentions Carlos as well. "By the way where is my painting you promised me?" Sheila remembers she did promise her a painting. She finished it, but she hasn't had the time to mail it.

"I have it and it's finished. With my sister being sick and in and out of the hospital I just haven't had the time to send it to you."

"How is Linda doing?"

"So far so good. Mom and I have taken her to the hospital four times within the last year or so. Every time we take her she's there for months at a time. The doctors don't seem to know what the problem is or how to fix or treat it. They seem to make things worse. She gets the best care from me at home."

"Hang in there and you're in my prayers. How's Mom?"

"She's good under the circumstances. I have to go. Carlos is calling."

"Okay. I'll Skype with you later. I want to know how things went with Carlos on the date. Bye!"

Sheila and Carlos decide to have an early dinner and catch a movie afterwards. Carlos offers to pick her up but she chooses to meet him at the restaurant instead. He suggests around 5:30 p.m. and she agrees. Sheila is trying to decide what to wear on the date with Carlos. She wants something that is comfortable and casual but cute too. Sheila asks her mom's opinion on the three outfits that she has put together. Her mom tells her which one she likes the best and puts it on. She tells her mom what Carlos has planned and where they'll be. Sheila figures her mom and Linda should be alright for a couple of hours. If there's an emergency they can call her cell phone. "Have fun and don't worry about us. If there's an emergency I'll call you."

"Okay. I'll try. I should be home by ten or eleven."

When she gets to the restaurant she sees Carlos. He looks really nice, but nervous. He's pacing back and forth outside in front of the door to the restaurant. As Sheila approaches him he freezes and stares at her for a few seconds. She wonders if he is going to say something or just stand there staring all night.

"You look wow!"

"Thank you. You don't look bad yourself." Carlos opens the door for Sheila as they enter the restaurant. They are seated right away. The restaurant is filled with very few people. Carlos pulls the seat out for Sheila. It doesn't take long for Sheila and Carlos to start talking. She asks him about the children. He talks about how she made quite the impression on them. Sheila can tell he adores and loves his children very much. They continue to talk throughout dinner. Before they know it they have missed the movie. They can't believe they have been talking for the last two hours or so. Sheila sees the hostess locking the door as their waitress comes to their table with the check saying they're closing. Carlos pays the check and he walks Sheila to her car.

"Maybe we could do this again and see a movie this time?"

"I would love to, Carlos. And tell your children I said hi."

Carlos leans in for a kiss, but he hesitates. He decides he shouldn't kiss her on their first date. He opens Sheila's car door and she climbs in thinking she wouldn't mind if he had kissed her sweetly. Carlos goes his way and Sheila heads home thinking about her date. She had a really nice time and found it very easy to talk to Carlos. It's been a while since Sheila had some fun. It's about time she did. When she arrives home both her mom and sister are anxious to know how the date went. Sheila tells them about the date. She tells them about the food, the conversation, and how they ended up missing the movie. She's beat so she hits the bed early.

Chapter 7

Sheila wakes up the next morning with a spring in her step. She notices the time. "Mom, why didn't you wake me? It's almost 10 a.m."

"You needed your rest. I wanted you to sleep in. I took care of Linda and all you have to do is her medicine."

"What about you?"

"I took my medicine and checked my sugar. It was good. So now you don't have to bug me." Sheila looks at her mom sternly knowing she's just messing with her. Her mom knows she only does it out of love and concern and starts grinning. Sheila figures this would be a good time to work on a new painting. She's had an idea for one for weeks. She always has lots of ideas floating around in her head. Something always seems to inspire her. Mostly nature inspires her. People not so much because she finds them to be cruel, irritating, aggravating, rude, inconsiderate, disrespectful, dishonest, and selfish. But Sheila knows that there are good people in the world. They're just few and far between. Sheila and her family are one of the few. Some people are so filled with hatred and anger in this world. It's easy to hate, but it's harder to love. As she gets older Sheila understands people less and less, so her mom tells her to stop trying and live her life the best way she knows how.

Her mom comes into her room to see the painting. She likes it and thinks it's very pretty so far. She loves the colors Sheila chose to use. Sheila's paintings make her mom smile and make her happy. "Don't you think we should start dinner?"

"Okay. I'm ready to quit painting for today. I'll go back to it later." It's been a few days since she heard from Carlos. She thought things went well on the date. But she has stuff to keep her busy. People are contacting her about her art and she has sold some more of it. Now Sheila is making a gallery website showcasing her art. While she's working on it she thinks Eliza is trying to Skype with her. And she is to her surprise.

"Hey, lady! What's up?"

"What's up with you and Carlos? How was the date?"

"I thought the date went really well. I don't know. I haven't heard from him in a week or so."

"I wouldn't worry. He's probably busy."

"I have a website so when you have time check it out. Tell me what you think and your painting is on the way."

"I'll believe it when I see it. How's Linda and your mom?"

"Good. Mom needs me right now so I have to go. Bye!"

"Bye! We'll chat later." Her mom needs help with Linda. While Sheila is helping her mom she reminds her not to eat or drink anything after midnight or in the morning because she's getting bloodwork done tomorrow. Sheila also reminds her of the appointment with her cardiologist to perform a stress test in a few days. Later that evening Sheila finally ships off the painting she promised Eliza. She still hasn't heard from Carlos and it has been a few weeks. The next day Sheila wakes up with a bad feeling. She's not exactly sure what it is, but she knows something is about to happen. And it's not good. Sheila is used to the bottom falling out. But she is reminded of the story of Job. Everything that could happen to him did, but he kept his faith in God who never forsaken him. And he and his family were rewarded in the end. Sheila's intuition has always been spot on. After Sheila and her mom finish cutting and edging the yard, Carlos pulls into the driveway. He compliments Sheila on the yard and she thanks him. They chat for a few minutes. She has the feeling something's up with him. He's acting awkward and strange. And then Carlos finally tells Sheila he's going to work it out with his exwife. Sheila wishes him good luck and hopes things work out for them.

"What did Carlos want?" She tells her mom.

"I'm sorry, sweetie!"

"That's alright, Mom. She's the mother of his children and if they can work it out they should."

"Let's go start dinner. I'm hungry!"

"Okay!" Sheila knows this is not the bad something that was going to happen. It's something else. Her mom's bloodwork came out good and today she gets the results from the stress test she did last week. Sheila goes with her to the doctor's office and prays that there is nothing wrong. She hopes the results are good. Her mom is not worried and thinks Sheila shouldn't be either. Sheila's prayers are answered. The doctor informs them the results are excellent and her mom should and needs to continue taking her medicine and monitoring her blood pressure. It wouldn't hurt being a little more active and exercising. As Sheila and her mom walk through the front door Linda is standing there.

"Is Mom okay? What did the doctor say?"

"I'm fine. She says I'm doing well and I need to exercise more. I told you there was nothing to worry about, Sheila!"

"You know me, Mom."

That evening she Skypes with Eliza. She asks her about Carlos. And Sheila explains the situation concerning Carlos. When it comes to men she doesn't have very good luck. Sheila believes things are going well and then she never hears from them again. "There's someone out there for you. You just haven't met him yet, but you will. I received the painting yesterday. And I love it. The website is cool too. Some of my friends and coworkers are interested."

"I hope you're right. Just have them email me or call me about my art. I sold some more of my art and I'm currently working on a painting now when I can find the time. So what's up with you?"

"I finished up my masters and I should receive it this weekend. And I also received a promotion which means attending more meetings and more paperwork. Now I'm teaching English to sixth graders as well as seventh graders. Other than that nothing much." She lets out a laugh. "My family and I are planning on coming down for a visit."

"Congrats and you know you love it and the kids. You can handle it. Let me know when you guys are coming down. It would be great to see you. I'll Skype with you later. I have to go. Bye!" Sheila still cannot shake this bad feeling. If it's not about her mom's health then what is it about? But she cannot figure it out. She knows something is about to happen. The next day Sheila finds some time to work on her painting. Sketching, drawing, and painting relax her. It makes Sheila feel less stressed.

Chapter 8

Sheila still has that bad feeling she can't shake. She notices that Linda doesn't look well. She asks her how she's feeling. Linda says she feels fine. Sheila takes her vitals which are good. A few days later Linda still doesn't look well. She feels tired, but her vitals are still good. The last thing Linda wants to do is go to emergency and Sheila feels the same way. Her mom and Sheila will just have to keep a close eye on Linda. Sheila receives an interesting call from a gallery owner. The owner has heard of Sheila's art and has seen her website. She is interested in showing some of Sheila's art in her gallery. She would like Sheila to email images of her art to her and then set up a meeting in the very near future with her to see her art and her in person. Sheila aggresses. Linda still is not looking good. She is complaining of pain and her vitals are not good. She is also running a high temperature as well. Sheila's mom says it's time to take her to emergency. They get in the car quickly and run Linda up to emergency. The ER is full of people. Sheila has a feeling they are going to be here for a while. After sitting in the ER for an hour or two the nurse calls Linda's name and takes her vitals. After they take her to a room the nurse draws her blood and asks for a urine sample. After waiting an hour for the doctor and the results Sheila's mom steps outside to warm up. They keep the hospital freezing cold to keep down germs. Sheila thinks to herself, Is it really necessary to keep the hospital that cold? After another couple of hours someone comes in to take xrays. Linda is getting more and more anxious as time goes by. Sheila tries her best to calm her. Finally after being there for a total of nine or ten hours the doctor comes in to explain the results. The doctor admits Linda and says she needs a blood transfusion. She also has an infection of some kind. Sheila goes outside to find her mom and explain the situation. They go back inside to check on Linda and let her know they'll be back in the morning. When they visit her the next day she looks very nervous and scared. They try to calm Linda down, but it's no use. They calm her down some. She sees the doctor, but she can't tell them what he said. He said a lot and she didn't understand half of it. The nurse on shift explains to Sheila and her mom what the doctor said. Sheila pretty much knows how it's going to go. The doctor or doctors won't let them know what's going on until they need consent to do a procedure or invasive test. They're going to have to set up a time to talk to the doctor or run him down. The doctor(s) won't listen to them or they'll end up making things worse. When Linda is discharged she will not be able to follow up with the doctors because they don't accept Medicaid.

Linda has been in the hospital for a week. Sheila and her mom have visited her every day. She looks better after having two blood transfusions, but she still has the infection for which they gave her antibiotics. They're concerned about her blood pressure, especially about her very high heart rate. Sheila tells them she's nervous and scared. The way doctors talk to her doesn't help the situation either, she mentions. Linda doesn't understand this doctor language. Most people don't understand this doctor language anyway but only another doctor does. She tells them they need to use simple plain English and choose their words carefully when speaking with her sister. Of course it is going just like Sheila thought it would. And this is Linda's fifth trip to the hospital. It's always stressful. Sheila and her mom do not like this hospital, but it's the closest one. They take turns visiting Linda. Sheila works on her art and helps her mom around the house and in the yard to keep her mind off of Linda. They do a lot of praying.

It has been almost two weeks and they still don't know what's wrong with Linda. Sheila wakes up with a bad feeling in her stomach. She wasn't going to visit her sister today, but she changes her mind. When Sheila and her mom arrive at the hospital they come to find Linda not in her room. The nurse informs them she has been moved to ICU. Shocked and stunned they quickly race to ICU where they are informed that Linda is in coma. She has swelling on the brain which they are trying to get to go down and her breathing started to fail along with her heart. After talking with the doctor her mom and Sheila spend a couple of hours with Linda. Then they go home and try to get some sleep that night. Both Sheila and her mom pray that night a long prayer to God. Every day they visit Linda and her condition stays the same. The swelling on her brain has not gotten worse, but it has not gone down either. Linda has been in coma for almost a month, and Sheila wonders if her sister will come out of this or will they have to pull the plug. Sheila has not brought this up to her mom. She's afraid to, but at some point if she doesn't come out of the coma they will have to make that decision.

Later that evening her mom and Sheila discuss pulling the plug. "I've been thinking about that too, Sheila. I was afraid to bring it up because I didn't know if you were ready to let your sister go. Maybe she'll come out of this. But only God knows."

"Mom, maybe we should wait before we pull the plug and see what happens. Are you prepared to pull the plug?"

"Yes. And are you? If there is no improvement within the next month or so then we'll pull the plug." Sheila agrees with that.

The next day Sheila hears from the gallery owner who would like to meet her and take a closer look at her pieces of art. She explains to the gallery owner that this is not a good time. Sheila explains to her that right now she is dealing with a family medical emergency and her mom needs her right now. The gallery owner hopes for the best and puts Sheila and her family in her prayers. But she conveys she would still love to meet her and see her art in person when the time is right. While her mom and Sheila are sitting with Linda at the hospital the doctor speaks with them about her condition. She's stable and her condition is the same, but he explains to them that there is a procedure he would like to do that would reduce the swelling. He would like to proceed with it tomorrow morning. Sheila's mom agrees to the procedure after talking it over with Sheila and signs the papers giving the doctor consent. The next morning they go to the hospital and sit in the waiting room during the procedure. When a couple of hours go by Sheila begins to get that strange, bad feeling. After five minutes or so she begins to not feel so good.

Her mom can tell there's something wrong with Sheila. "Are you Okay? You don't look too good."

"I'm fine. I have a feeling there's something wrong." Her mom puts her arms around Sheila's shoulders and squeezes her. She lays her head on her mom's shoulder and her mom lays her head on top of hers.

"If there is a problem the doctor or someone would let us know. Everything is Okay." Soon the doctor comes out with a very grim look on his face. He tells them Linda didn't make it. There were complications and her heart stopped. They couldn't revive her. After a few moments he says that he's sorry for their loss and if there's anything they need let them know and he leaves.

Chapter 9

After the shock goes away her mom and Sheila discuss the funeral plans later that evening. After giving it some thought they decide not to have a funeral. Linda didn't know very many people. The only friend she had was Sheila. They decide to have Linda's body cremated also. Sheila realizes that night Linda isn't here anymore. The only person she has left is her mom. And she doesn't know how much longer she'll have her. She's in her seventies with health problems of her own that are manageable and controlled. Sheila does worry quite a bit. Then she hears that soft, kind voice whisper, "I have not and will not forsake you. You are not alone and have faith and trust in me. Put your mom and you in God's unchanging hands."

In the morning Sheila Skypes with Eliza. She explains what has happened to Linda. Eliza seems shocked and tries to console her. She gives Sheila words of encouragement. Later that day Sheila goes to the hospital for her mom to sign papers to release Linda's body to the funeral home. A couple days later Sheila and her mom go to the funeral home to make arrangements for Linda's cremation. Sheila finds a beautiful urn online that she orders and hopes will arrive soon. The urn arrives in the mail just in time. The funeral home calls to let them know Linda's ashes are ready to be picked up along with the death certificates. They go the next morning to pick up Linda's ashes and decide to put the urn next to her father's urn on the mantle in the family room. Sheila straightens out Linda's affairs for her mom; however, there is not a lot to straighten out. It takes her a few days to get it all done. Sheila remembers when her dad passed away. It took her weeks or maybe months to straighten out her dad's affairs for her mom.

It's been a couple of months since Linda passed away. While Sheila's working in the yard with her mom it dawns on her what is she going to do now. For most of her life she has taken care of her family and friends. She thought about going back to college, but what would she study? She knows it will not be medicine, but maybe art. But she doesn't have the money to go back to school either. She could try job hunting, but it's been ten years or more since she looked for one. The way they do things are different. Maybe she'll have better luck this time. Sheila's also concerned about her mom. She's getting up there in age and Sheila wants to be there if she needs something. All of sudden she hears that soft, kind voice whisper, "Have faith. Through me all things are possible." While planting a few flowers Sheila turns her head in the direction of her mom who is talking to one of their neighbors.

She hears the neighbor say, "Sorry for your loss and if you need anything let me know." Sheila was hoping she wouldn't hear those words, sorry for your loss and so on, for a while. Sheila and her mom heard it enough when her dad passed away. Sheila's mom was tired of hearing it too, but she tells her that's what people say. They mean well most of the time. The next day Sheila gets on her computer searching for job openings, and pretty much comes up empty. For the next week Sheila works on her resume and searches for job openings on her computer. Her resume isn't very impressive. She has little work experience, and she wishes her life experience counted. Sheila makes copies of her resume and drops them off at numerous places and applies to jobs online. Later that evening during dinner Sheila's mom asks her how the job search is going.

"I don't know. I haven't heard from anyone yet. My resume isn't that impressive and I have very little work experience."

"It's only been a few weeks. Once you get a job interview they'll see how smart you are and how much of a hard worker you are."

"Maybe you're right."

Sheila's mom can tell there's something on her mind. "Sheila, what's wrong?"

"Nothing."

Her mom doesn't believe her. While they continue to eat dinner her mom gives it some thought. "I'll be fine, so you don't have to worry about me being at home by myself."

"What if you fall in the garden, in the house, have a heart attack, or a stroke."

"I take my medication with your help and you make sure I eat healthy. You help me to stay active and I'll make sure you're here when I do something crazy. I can call you on your cell phone if I need you."

"You promise?"

"I promise. You won't be working all day and night. Have you heard from the gallery owner? Maybe you should call her."

"I forgot about her. I think I will. I was thinking about taking some art classes to improve on my art."

"That's not a bad idea. If you can find some affordable classes I might be able to help you pay for them." While they are finishing up dinner, Sheila's mom mentions going to church this Sunday. Sheila thinks that would be nice. The last time they went to church it was a week after her dad's funeral. It felt strange and different. The congregation had gotten smaller and most of their friends had left the church to join other churches or passed away. Sheila and her mom did not care too much for the new pastor. Sheila's church friend had told her that this pastor was voted out by the congregation. She told Sheila that she and her mom are going to like this pastor. He's a good man and nice. Hopefully this one will stick around. Sheila thinks it wouldn't hurt to check it out and she misses going to church.

Chapter 10

That morning Sheila and her mom put their Sunday best on and head out the door. As they walk through the church doors they hear a familiar voice. "I would know that big, beautiful, and classy hat anywhere, child!" They turn around with big grins on their faces. It's Mrs. Sutton, a family friend that Sheila's family has known since the first day they joined the church. Sheila's mom and Mrs. Sutton give each other a big warm hug. Her grandchildren appear from around the corner with huge smiles on their faces and practically rush Sheila all at once. They all sit together. As Sheila sits and listens to the sermon and the choir sings, it still feels strange being here, but it feels right too. They did like this pastor. When church service ends Sheila and her mom go out to dinner with Mr. and Mrs. Sutton and their family. They catch up. They talk about what's going on with the church. The next day Sheila calls the gallery owner to set up a meeting. Sheila is excited about the meeting as she gets prepared and ready to go. Sheila's mom can tell and is happy for her. It's been a while since she saw Sheila glow or shine. As Sheila walks into the gallery she takes everything in including the atmosphere and the paintings. She thinks the paintings are amazing and beautiful. Sheila is brought back to reality by a voice in the distance. "Ms. Jones?"

"Oh, yes." As they walk towards each other the gallery owner holds out her hand and they shake.

"I'm Ms. Emily La Rue. Nice to finally meet you."

"Thank you for taking an interest. I was just admiring your gallery and the art."

"Shall we have a seat and start the meeting?" As Ms. La Rue is looking at Sheila's work she is asking her questions. Sheila also hands over her resume and basically tells Ms. La Rue her life story starting from college to her sister's passing. Ms. La Rue doesn't speak for a few moments. She has a shocked look on her face as if she does not know exactly how to respond. "Well, that is an amazing story and you are very talented."

"Thank you, but I feel that I can improve on my art. I'm thinking about taking some art classes."

"Not only talented but smart too. We have workshops here and classes. And I would love to show your work starting with these pieces you showed me."

"Thank you again, Ms. La Rue! I really appreciate that!" As Sheila gets up and turns to leave she sees this quiet, unassuminglooking young man in a suit. She can't help but to feel a kind, gentle spirit emanating from him. She wonders how long he's been standing there. As Ms. La Rue walks Sheila out an idea comes to her mind.

"I also need some help around the gallery. It would be a wonderful experience for you. You can start tomorrow and we can work out your schedule then. Is 9 a.m. good for you?" Sheila is stunned and not quite sure what to say. But she better say something soon.

"Okay, Ms. La Rue." As they approach the door she introduces Sheila to the young man.

"This is Mr. James Logan. And this is Ms. Sheila Jones. I'm going to be displaying some of her art."

"Hello, Ms. Jones. Very nice to make your acquaintance."

"Hello, Mr. Logan. Likewise." As they shake hands their eyes lock on each other for a few moments. Sheila notices that Mr. Logan has nice eyes that are kind. Mr. Logan also notices that Sheila has a beautiful, warm, and inviting smile. They both feel a strong connection between them. Then they realize they're both still holding hands and let go fairly quickly. "Okay, Ms. La Rue. I'll see you tomorrow and thank you again for the opportunity." After Sheila leaves Mr. Logan and Ms. La Rue go sit down at her desk and start chatting.

"So, you're showing a new artist?"

"Yes. And she's very talented. She reminds me of you." Ms. La Rue has a feeling about these two. She felt something undeniable between them.

"How so?"

"Family is important to both of you. You're both very smart and try to do the right thing. You're both good people. I actually see her owning her own gallery someday."

"Shouldn't you see first if any of her art sells?"

"I have a good feeling about her. She has tremendous potential and talent. She's a rare special diamond."

"You got all that from a twenty or thirty minute conversation?" "So, you were listening in, huh? Well, I was right about you. So anyway, what brings you here today?"

"I was having lunch nearby so I thought I would check in and see how things are going."

"The gallery is doing well. If you want to the office is open and you can look over the books. Just remember to lock up the office when you're done."

"Okay. Mrs. Jones's art is breathtaking." Once Mr. Logan finishes up in Ms. La Rue's office he sits on a bench looking through Sheila's paintings, one in particular more than the others.

Chapter 11

Sheila can't wait to tell her mom the good news. The minute she walks through the door she tells her mom everything. Her mom can't believe all this happened from one initial meeting. This is a wonderful opportunity for Sheila and her mom's so happy for her. Her mom mentions to Sheila she needs her help in the yard, so she changes her clothes. Later that evening they make dinner and talk about the rest of the day while eating.

Sheila has been working at the gallery for a few months now enjoying every minute of it. Her art has improved since she has been attending workshops and art classes. She's learning quite a bit from Ms. La Rue who would like to display some more of Sheila's art. While Sheila is putting up some new artwork on the wall something comes to Ms. La Rue. She jumps out her chair and steps out of her office. "Sheila, would you like to put on your own art showcase?"

Sheila has a stunned look on her face. She's not sure how to respond. "I don't know, Ms. La Rue. I'm not quite sure that I'm ready."

"I believe you are and I'll help you put it together and everything."

"That would be great! Thank you!"

"Can I come by your home this weekend and we can get started?"

"That will be fine." When Sheila gets off of work she tells her mom the news. Her mom is excited and believes this is wonderful. But Sheila isn't so sure. She's a little scared and nervous. Sheila doesn't like attention and tends to shy away from it. Her mom is also curious about the gallery owner whom she's looking forward to meeting. Sheila talks about her all the time. Sheila's mom answers the door after hearing the doorbell ring.

She comes to the conclusion this has to be Ms. La Rue. "You must be Ms. La Rue. Come in!"

"And you must be Mrs. Evelynn Jones, Sheila's mom. Call me Emily."

"Okay. And call me Evie."

"You have a wonderful daughter."

"Thank you. I think she is pretty great too."

Suddenly Sheila comes around the corner. "I have all my paintings out over here!"

"Sheila, where are your manners!"

"Sorry, Mom. Let me take your coat. Would you like something to drink?"

"No, thank you. I would like to get started though."

"Well, I'll let you get to it. And you are welcome to stay for dinner. I'll be in the den if you need me for something." Sheila stands there nervously as Ms. La Rue looks over her work.

As Ms. La Rue gives Sheila suggestions and ideas she notices her nervous energy. "Sheila, you'll do great. I believe in you and your art." That seems to calm her nerves. As they are finishing up Sheila's mom tells them dinner is done. As they eat Ms. La Rue tells them all about herself. Sheila thought she knew everything about her, but there is a lot more to her. She went to college where she majored in art history and studied abroad in France for a year where she learned to speak French. She also learned to speak Spanish and Italian as well. She painted some, but felt she could never be as good as the greats. She traveled and visited parts of Europe, Asia, and Egypt while working for an art museum. She got weary of that life and decided to put down roots. She always had an eye for art and she knew great art when she saw it. She decided to open an art gallery. She went to business school and the rest is history. Her life has been good, but the only regret she has is never being blessed with children. Ms. La Rue and Sheila's mom are similar in many ways. They both have good hearts, are friendly, speak their minds, are opinionated, and love flowers. Sheila's mom gives her the grand tour of the garden which she loves. "Well, I should go. I pretty much wore out my welcome."

"No you didn't. It was a pleasure and I enjoyed it very much." "Me too. Sheila I'll see you at work and Evie I'll hopefully see you at the art show."

"Absolutely! I wouldn't miss it."

Chapter 12

It's the night of the art show. Sheila is nervous, but excited at the same time. Sheila's mom is trying to calm her nerves while they're getting ready for the show. They decide to leave early just in case Ms. La Rue needs help setting up. As they get ready to leave Sheila's mom suddenly stops and stands there looking at her daughter with tremendous pride and love. When she realizes her mom is not right behind her Sheila turns around. "Mom, what's wrong? Are you okay?"

"Oh, I'm fine. You look beautiful. Let's go. We don't want to be late." As they walk into the gallery Sheila can't believe it or describe what she's feeling in words at this moment. Both Sheila and her mom stand there frozen taking in the art surrounding them and everything.

Ms. La Rue walks up behind them. "What are you guys doing here so early? By the way you look amazing."

"Thank you. We thought you might need help."

"Well, you came just in time to help me hang the rest of Sheila's art. Everything else is set up." They finish hanging up the rest of the art with Ms. La Rue's direction and now it's time to open the doors to let the public in. Quite a few people are coming in. Ms. La Rue pulls Sheila to the middle of the room. But she's not sure what's happening. "I would like to introduce you to the artist, Ms. Sheila Jones. Thank you for coming and I hope you enjoy the art." Ms. La Rue whispers to Sheila to go mingle, but she won't let go of her. "It'll be okay. Just be yourself." Finally she slowly lets go, takes a deep breath, and starts talking to people. Ms. La Rue takes Evie's arm. "Let me show you around. She'll be okay." As they begin to walk away she looks back at Sheila.

"I know." Ms. La Rue is giving Evie the grand tour while Sheila is mingling. It's not as scary as she thought it would be. She's meeting some interesting and nice people. She is enjoying herself quite a bit. As she is talking to a small group of people Sheila notices a young man who looks like James. She excuses herself and as she walks towards him he doesn't take his eyes off of her.

"James, what are you doing here? This is a surprise."

After a few moments he finally says something. "You look absolutely breathtaking."

Sheila is taken aback by his response. "Thank you."

"Oh, Ms. La Rue asked me to help her set up and I wanted to see the rest of your art. I really like this one. It reminds me of my mom. This was one of her favorite flowers."

"I'm glad you like it."

James notices Ms. La Rue waving her hand at them. "I think Ms. La Rue is trying to get your attention. So, I'll let you go." Sheila turns her head and sees Ms. La Rue approaching them. She thanks James for coming and then politely excuses herself. As Sheila walks away James stands there sweetly, lovingly gazing at her until she is out of his view. After a few more hours of mingling and Ms. La Rue introducing Sheila to certain people she is ready for the night to be over. Finally it is the end of the art show. Sheila, her mom, and James stay to help Ms. La Rue straighten and clean up. They talk about how well the night went and the art. When Sheila's head hits the pillows she falls straight off to sleep.

A few days later James pops into the gallery with a beautiful bouquet of flowers. "If you're looking for Ms. La Rue she's not here right now. She's at a doctor's appointment. Those are lovely flowers."

"Since Ms. La Rue loves flowers so much I bring her some from my dad's garden every so often." Sheila often wondered where the flowers came from. Every week or so she would see a different fresh bouquet. She just assumed Ms. La Rue bought them from a flower shop. They are breathtaking and so vibrant. James's dad obviously has a green thumb like Sheila's mom. He's curious as to what her favorite flower is. She doesn't really have one. She likes anything that's vibrant, colorful, and unique. She loves yellow roses. James looks down at his watch and realizes he's late for a meeting. "Well, I have to run. Tell Ms. La Rue I'll talk with her later." Then James rushes off.

The next day Sheila and her mom find a big, beautiful vase of yellow roses with a note that reads:

I hope you enjoy these. I thought you might truly appreciate their beauty.
Sincerely, James.

Sheila's mom notices a big smile come across her face. She hands her mom the card to read.

"Mom, thank you for helping me out at work today."

"You're welcome, sweetie. Just tell me what to do boss."

"Mom, I'm not your boss!"

"For today you are. James seems like a nice guy and cute too."

Sheila quickly tries to change the subject. "I hope Ms. La Rue feels better."

"Me too. So what do you think about James?"

"I think we should get to work. Mom, will you hand me those paintings please?" Her mom seems to have no choice but to drop the subject.

Chapter 13

As the weeks progress Ms. La Rue gives Sheila more responsibilities and shows her how to keep the books/records and how her office is set up and runs. She gives Sheila access to her office and a second set of keys to the gallery. Sheila has noticed that Ms. La Rue has been missing a day or two of work here and there, but now she is missing weeks. Sheila is getting that strange feeling again that something isn't right. She feels like something is going to happen soon. She doesn't exactly know what it is, but she knows it's not good. Sheila's mom helps her out when she can at work. And to her surprise so does James as a favor to Ms. La Rue. She has been working closely with him for the last few weeks now. He doesn't say much. He's quiet and does what Sheila asks. She is also learning a lot on the business side from James. He seems very intelligent also. She doesn't exactly know what he does for a living. Sometimes he looks at this one painting in particular intensely and on occasion she catches him writing in a black leather notebook. Sheila doesn't really know what to make of him. James is a mystery to her. It's one that she wouldn't mind solving; however, her track record with guys isn't that great. Things go well at first and then it goes astray. The guy is a jerk or he doesn't know what he truly wants or they want different things. They're not compatible or on the same wavelength one can say. All that the last guy wanted was sex and not a relationship. Sheila didn't want that, so she nipped it in the bud before anything got started. Sheila wants more than that. She wants someone to go out with on a date to lunch or dinner and have good conversation with. Someone she can chill with at the movies, the park, or at home eating dinner or watching a movie on DVD. Someone she can get to know and if it blossoms into a relationship that's great. If not Sheila has hopefully gained a good friend or not. That's why Sheila is hesitant to get into a relationship one can say. Guys today just want to have sex. They don't even want to get to know you as a person before they're trying to get into your pants. At this point she has accepted the fact that her chances of being married are slim to none and she's fine with that. She has the ability to and can take care of herself. She's a very capable woman. She can always adopt. There are children in the world who need loving homes. Sheila is daydreaming at the desk until she hears a small voice. "Excuse me, ma'am. I'm looking for my Uncle James."

"He's in the back. You can go back there."

"Okay. Thank you, ma'am." The little girl dashes off to the back and then an old man comes in right after her. "Hello! You must be Sheila. I'm James's father, Mr. Logan. The art show was beautiful."

"Nice to meet you and thank you. I don't recall seeing you there, but there were quite a few people." Sheila mentions the yellow roses his son gave her. They talk about flowers and his garden. Mr. Logan bought the painting that his son liked so much at the art show. They talk about her mom's garden and how they have that in common. Shortly James and the little girl emerge from the back.

"Hey, Dad. Have you met Sheila?"

"Yes, I have. When should I pick up Samantha?"

"I would say in about two hours. We're going to the park and have lunch."

"Can Ms. Sheila come with us, Uncle James?"

"If she wants to."

"Sure. It's been a while since I've been to the park." Samantha hugs her grandpa goodbye.

"It was very nice talking to you, Sheila. And hopefully I'll be seeing you again soon."

"It was nice chatting with you too, Mr. Logan." As Mr. Logan leaves he looks back at his son with a big grin across his face as if he knows a secret. And then the three of them head out to the park. When they arrive at the park James pulls out a picnic basket from the back seat. They sit down at one of the picnic tables close to the playground equipment. He pulls out sandwiches, potato salad, and fruit.

"I made the sandwiches and grandpa made the salad."

"They look good. And I can't wait to have one." Sheila takes a bite. "You did an excellent job. And it taste very good."

"What do you say, Samantha?"

"Thank you."

"How old are you, Samantha?"

"I'm nine years old."

"Are you sure? I bet you're really twentyfive or thirty." Samantha lets out a giggle. "The potato salad is good too. Do you help your grandpa in the kitchen a lot?"

"Yes, ma'am. I'm his helper. He can cook, but my uncle not so much."

"Wait a minute! I did cut the fruit."

"Well you did an excellent job cutting the fruit." Then all three of them start laughing. Samantha runs off to play on the slide. James and Sheila start walking towards a bench and sit. While watching Samantha play they start talking. "She's adorable and very smart."

"Thank you. She's a lot like her mom, my sister. I overheard some of your interview with Ms. La Rue. My mom had Alzheimer's and Parkinson's too. I helped my dad as much as possible take care of her to the end."

"What about your sister? Didn't she help too?"

"As much as she could. She had her own family and a job. A couple years ago Samantha lost her parents in a car accident. My dad really couldn't take care of her by himself."

"So you take care of Samantha now? She's great. You're doing a fantastic job."

"Of course my dad helps me." They talk about how their parents would wonder off and how they would get confused. They had to watch them carefully 24/7 just about as the disease progressed. It was stressful and hard. The hardest part for them was to see their parents sick and become someone they didn't recognize. His mom was so sure of herself and full of life. She wasn't scared of anything or she wouldn't let it show. She was funny, smart, beautiful, and kind. Sheila's dad was quiet, smart, and handsome. If you needed something he wouldn't hesitate to say yes. He was always learning, improving himself, and active. But they both hold on to the good memories and the people they were before they got sick. When James lost his sister he also lost his best friend. He misses her and her husband. They all do. He believes his faith in God got him and his family through it. He prays for guidance and strength to get him through the day.

Samantha runs up and grabs them by the arms pulling them up off the bench. "Are you guys going to play or talk the whole time?" Sheila and Samantha go down the slide together a few times. Even James goes down the slide once or twice. They go on the swings as well. Sheila pushes Samantha for a bit and then James pushes Sheila for a while. They talk and laugh. This feels right. Then James looks down at his wrist and jumps up.

"We should go. Your grandpa is waiting." They pack everything up and head back to the gallery. James's dad is sitting in the car with the door open when they pull into the parking lot. James quickly gets out the car and grabs the picnic basket. Samantha grabs her stuff. "Sorry we're late, Dad. I guess time got away from me."

"I hope you weren't waiting too long, Mr. Logan."

"That's all right. I haven't been waiting too long and it looks like you guys had fun." Samantha's grinning from ear to ear nodding yes. "Well, son, we'll see you at home. Bye!" As they leave Sheila unlocks the gallery. They work for a few more hours and both head home.

The next day Sheila's mom comes to work with her. While they're working Sheila tells her mom about the day she spent at the park with James and Samantha. The whole time her mom notices how Sheila's face lights up and she can't stop smiling. "Maybe you should go out on a date with James."

"I'm pretty sure he probably has a girlfriend. He's not interested in me anyway."

"You don't know that for a fact and if James did I doubt he would be spending so much time here. He seems like a really good guy."

"Usually the good ones are taken and it doesn't work out anyway. He's only helping out as a favor to Ms. La Rue. I don't want to get involved with anyone right now. I just want to focus on my art."

"If all the good ones are taken you would be too. God has someone out there for you."

"I was thinking we could go out for dinner."

"Sounds good to me."

"You have an appointment with your heart doctor tomorrow."

"Okay. You're coming with me, right? If you're not with me she always asks me where you're at."

"Your doctors know you very well and they know I'll make sure you'll do what they tell you to."

"Are you saying I'm hard headed and is that a yes?"

"Yes to both and it runs in the family."

Chapter 14

Sheila is awoken by a loud ring. After a few seconds she realizes it's the phone. She answers it still half asleep. "It's James."

"Hi, James. Can't it wait tell I get to the gallery?"

"No, that's why I'm calling. Ms. La Rue passed away early this morning." Sheila doesn't say a word. She's stunned. "The memorial service is next week on Monday and the lawyer needs to talk to us about her last will and testament."

"Okay. I guess I'll see you at the service." Still stunned Sheila hangs up the phone and rolls out of bed. She finds her mom in the kitchen making coffee. To her Sheila doesn't look quite right.

"Honey, are you Okay?"

"That was James." A small grin comes across her mom's face.

"Ms. La Rue just died." The grin disappears but Sheila's mom doesn't look surprised.

"What do you want for breakfast?"

"You knew something was wrong?"

"Maybe I did."

"Why didn't you tell me?"

"Well, she made me promise not to tell you. You're always taking care of people you love and she didn't want you to worry about her I guess. I need your help in the yard. One or both of us needs to go grocery shopping."

"Okay. I need to check your blood glucose level. Did you eat anything yet and have you taken your medicine?"

"No and I was getting ready to take it now."

Sheila calls James the day before the service to get directions to the church. When Sheila and her mom arrive at the service she sees James, his father, and Samantha standing outside the church doors. As Sheila and her mom get out the car they meet them. Sheila introduces her mom to James's father and Samantha. They walk inside the church and it is full of people. Towards the front there are several paintings and in the center there is a table dressed with beautiful flowers and an urn. She doesn't recognize anyone except for a few people. She thinks they were at her art show. Right after the service an older man in a suit approaches them. "Ms. Jones and Mr. Logan? I'm Ms. La Rue's lawyer, Mr. Wilkerson. We can talk in the pastor's office. He said we could use it. It shouldn't take long."

"We'll wait out here for you guys, son."

The lawyer shows them to the pastor's office. Mr. Wilkerson takes the chair behind the pastor's desk while Sheila and James take the two in front of his desk. The lawyer does not hesitate and dives right in. "Ms. La Rue did not have any family. Both her parents are dead as well as her siblings. She was never married nor had any kids. She basically left everything to you. What I mean by that is she left the gallery to Ms. Jones. The estate she left to you and Mr. Logan. She also had a life insurance policy worth $100,000. She named you two the beneficiaries leaving Ms. Jones $70,000 and Mr. Logan $30,000. She also gave her ashes to Ms. Jones. One last thing, she wrote a letter for each of you that might help explain things better." He hands Sheila and James each an envelope with a business card. "If you have any questions or need help with something let me know." As the lawyer gets up to leave, Sheila and James sit there confused and stunned for several minutes.

Then the door opens. It's the pastor. "Is everything okay?" They both nod their heads yes; however, it doesn't look like they're okay to the pastor. "Well, your family is waiting outside. They were getting concerned."

"Thank you, pastor. We should go and let you have your office back." James pulls the chair out for Sheila.

As they leave the pastor thinks to himself, What a nice sweet couple. "You and your wife are welcome to come back anytime and attend Sunday service." Sheila and James look at each other and start laughing.

On the way home as the shock wears off Sheila tells her mom what the lawyer said. Her mom doesn't seem so shocked. "Let me guess you knew about this too."

Life's Unexpected Blessings

"Honestly, no. I'm not surprised. I knew she was sick and it didn't look like she was getting any better. She didn't tell me anything about her will." The rest of the ride home they didn't say a word. Sheila's mom could tell that she was in deep thought. Sheila stares at the urn wondering to herself why she left everything to her and James. The first thing Sheila does when she arrives home is reads her letter.

Dear Sheila,

Please don't be mad at your mom. I made her not tell you I was sick. If you knew, you would be taking care of me. But I didn't want that. But what I needed and wanted you were doing. You were taking care of and running my gallery. I never had children, but if I did have one I would hope she was just like you. To me you're like a daughter that I got to pass down my knowledge of art to and other things. I know you already have a wonderful mom who did a fantastic job. If you decide not to keep the gallery my lawyer is instructed to sell it and is required to give you the money from the transaction. If you do decide to keep it, I want you to make it your own. You can change it and rename it. It's yours. Art is part of you. It's in your soul. As for my estate that is up to you and James as what to do with it. You can sell it and split the money 50/50 or keep it. If you and James ever get married consider it my wedding gift. The two of you can decide what paintings you want, flowers, etc. As for my ashes I'll trust you'll know what to do with them. I have faith in you.

Love,

Ms. Emily La Rue

Sheila hears a knock at her bedroom door. She turns her head to see her mom in the doorway. She comes in and sits next to Sheila on the bed. She puts her arm around Sheila's shoulder as she lays her head on her mom's shoulder. "Are you okay?"

"Yeah, I guess. Why did she leave me the gallery?"

"I don't know, honey. I think she honestly cared about and truly thought the world of you. You can say she kind of adopted you. She really didn't have anyone she could leave her stuff to. I guess she thought you and James would be the best people to leave her belongings to."

"I don't know if I'm even capable of running the gallery."

"Well, you did run it by yourself for several months."

"Yeah, but I had you and James helping me."

"Yes, but you were the boss. You still have me and you'll always have me. Whatever you decide I will support and help you. You and James have to make the decision about the estate and the money is yours to do with what you wish."

"Thanks, Mom! I love you!"

"I'm hungry. I'm ready to eat dinner."

"Mom, you made dinner?"

"Don't look so surprised! I still know my way around the kitchen. I just don't like being in it." They both start laughing. That night Sheila is having trouble sleeping. Ms. La Rue's letter didn't make things any clearer. She does not know what to do about the gallery. Is she making a huge mistake if she keeps it? Should she just have the lawyer sell it and take the money? Can she really run the gallery on her own? What should she do with her estate and her ashes? She finally falls off to sleep after a couple of hours.

She hears a soft, kind voice whisper, "Have faith. I will be with you and guide your steps. Ask for wisdom you shall receive it. Ask for guidance you shall receive it. Ask for strength you shall receive it. Pray for these things they shall be given."

The next morning Sheila wakes up with a clear mind. Sheila and her mom are giving the house a serious cleaning while playing music. They like to play music while they work. To them it makes work go faster and more fun. At that moment she tells her mom what she decided about the gallery. Sheila decides to keep it and run it herself. She also wants to use some of the money to go back to school and earn her business degree. The business degree should help her run it better. She's still going to continue her art classes. Sheila has all these ideas for the gallery. She wants to change the décor and add a garden shop using her mom's plants. Her mom is always saying she has too many plants around the house. She's always starting new plants from the clippings or trimmings. She wants her to help her with the gallery, but mainly wants her to take charge of the garden shop. Sheila also wants to introduce other mediums of art besides just paintings and make the gallery more kid friendly. Her mom can tell she's excited about these ideas. Her ideas sound really good. One thing her mom has learned about her baby is never to doubt or underestimate her. Her mom figures Sheila has nothing to lose. She said she would support Sheila and she does. "Well, what do you think, Mom?"

"I said I would support your decision. If this is what you truly want to do I say go for it."

"The estate I'm not sure about. I want to see it first before I make any decisions."

"It's beautiful on the inside and on the outside."

"Are there any other secrets you're keeping?"

"Isn't your mother allowed a few secrets? I tell you the important things."

"I guess." Sheila's mom hears a song she likes and starts dancing. Sheila starts giggling and dancing herself. Then the two of them start doing the bump. A week or two later they go to view the estate. As they pull up to the estate Sheila's jaw drops. Her mom was right. It's absolutely breathtaking. The house isn't small, but by no means is it a mansion. The yard is full of shrubs and all kinds of flowers. Ms. La Rue never acted like she had a lot of money. Sheila doesn't know what to say. As they get out of the car she sees the front door opening. Samantha runs out and gives Sheila a huge hug.

She looks up to see James standing in the doorway. They step inside the house and it's just as breathtaking as the outside of the house. She catches a glimpse of the backyard through a window. It's quite large and full of shrubs and flowers just like the front. "I was going to call you. My dad is in the back. Let me show you guys around."

"Thank you, James, but I've already seen it. You should show Sheila around and talk though. I think I'll take a look around the garden in the back. Would you like to come with me, Samantha?" She looks over at Sheila. "I'll be out there when your Uncle and I are done looking at the house."

"Yes, ma'am." She takes Mrs. Jones's hand and they go outside. James proceeds to show Sheila the house. First he shows her the kitchen. It's spacious with a long aisle in the middle and a long counter at which to sit. There's a lot of room to move around. There's also a dining table off to the side that looks out into the front yard. Sheila loves it. Then he shows her the bedrooms which each have a view of the back yard. But Sheila falls in love with the art studio. This would be ideal for her to create art. "I guess that concludes the tour. So, what do you think?"

"The house is beautiful."

"We could sell it and split the money 50/50. This house looks like it could be worth quite a bit of money." Sheila's not quite sure about selling it. James is probably right about the house being worth quite a lot. "Sheila, what are you thinking?"

"I would hate to sell it and the new owners end up not taking care of it including the yard. I can see that Ms. La Rue put a lot of work and love into this home and her garden. She left us some money in her will. Do you or I really need the money?"

"You do have a point."

"We could keep it and I could buy you out. Or we could coown it and share it."

James stands there for a few moments thinking. "Or I could buy you out instead."

"You could if you really wanted the house and I didn't. But I haven't made up my mind yet."

James stands there silent for a few moments. "I think we should both give it some more thought and discuss it some more later."

"Okay. I agree." James opens the door for Sheila and they proceed to the backyard.

Sheila's curious about a few things. She has the source walking right next to her, so why not ask him what she wants to know. "Were you close to Ms. La Rue?"

"Yes. I knew her ever since I was little. My sister and I considered her family. She was like an aunt. My mom and her met in college and became best friends. They stayed close to the end."

"Why did she leave us the estate? What does she want us to do with it?"

"I'm not sure."

"Didn't she tell you in her letter?"

"Not exactly. She considered me to be the closest thing to a son. And it was up to us to make the decision about how to handle the estate. You ask a lot of questions."

"If you don't ask, then how do you gain knowledge or understanding?"

"Once again another good point made." In the distance they can see their parents talking and Samantha chasing butterflies.

As they get close Sheila sees a beautiful gazebo sitting in the middle of the garden. "Sheila, isn't it breathtaking? I want to look around the garden some more. Then we can go."

"Sure, Mom. Hi, Mr. Logan. You're welcome to any of the plants."

"Thank you, Sheila. I might take you up on the offer."

"Dad, you ready to go?"

"I think I want to look around the garden some more too." Sheila and James go sit in the gazebo and talk some more. Sheila finds out he's an accountant, but went to college and majored in architecture. He minored in business. He actually designed and built this gazebo. They talk about the gallery too. Sheila tells him about her plans for the gallery and how she's going back to school to acquire a business degree. James offers his help with the classes if she needs it. She might take him up on his offer.

Sheila hears her mom's voice in the distance. "I'm ready!" On the way home they stop by Home Depot to pick out paint and the grocery store to pick up a few things.

Chapter 15

The next day Sheila attends her first class. As she is walking on campus it feels strange to her. It's been nearly fifteen years since she's been in school. But it also feels good. She's enjoying the classes and meeting new people. Her classes will also be online so some of her time will be freed up. The next weekend Sheila and her mom start working on the gallery. While they're getting the supplies and paint out of the car Sheila notices a car pull up. James and his family get out of the car. Sheila and her mom are surprised. "I thought you guys would like some help." James looks different. Sheila's used to seeing him in a suit or dress clothes. But he looks pretty good in street clothes.

"Sure, thanks! We would appreciate that a lot. Could you guys grab the rest of the stuff?" As they walk in the gallery Sheila starts organizing them. Sheila and Samantha paint one section a purple shade of color. James paints another section a green shade of color while his father and Sheila's mother paint the last section a yellow shade of color. While they're working Sheila plays music. She and Samantha start dancing and giggling. She teaches her how to do the bump. Everyone starts laughing and smiling and soon join in except James.

"Uncle James come on!"

"Yeah, son, come join us!"

"I don't dance." They continue to paint and groove. James's dad and Sheila's mom talk while they paint.

"What do you think of my son?"

"He seems like a very nice young man. What do you think about my daughter?"

"She seems like a very nice, smart young lady. Now what do you think about them together?"

"I already went there. She wants to focus on the gallery and her art. She's stubborn and once her mind is set you can't change it."

"Sounds like my son. They would be good together."

"I think so too, but they're grown adults. I think we should just let nature take its course."

"We can help it along a little."

"How?"

"I think we should go get some ice cream or lunch and leave the two of them here. And we take our time."

"I am a little hungry. Okay." James's dad lets them know they're going out to get lunch and maybe some ice cream. They'll bring them some food back. Samantha tags along which they were hoping. Sheila and James continue to work. They start wondering what's taking them so long. James calls his dad's cell phone. Sheila takes a little break and notices James's leather notebook on the desk. She starts looking through it. His designs are stunning and unique.

"My dad says the restaurant is busy. It might take another hour or so."

"This is what you were doing in the notebook. Your sketches or designs are beautiful. I love those benches."

A slow tempo song starts to play. James holds out his hand. "May I have this dance?"

"I thought you didn't dance."

"This is more my speed and I didn't say I couldn't dance." Sheila takes his hand and James pulls her in close. They start moving and almost gliding across the floor. "Could you build three or four benches and a small metal gazebo for the gallery? I'm thinking they would look nice in here. I'll pay you."

"I can't seem to say no to you. It'll take me a few weeks. Maybe a little longer and you don't need to pay me."

"Thank you. There has to be something I can do for you."

"You can stop talking for five minutes." James looks into her eyes. Then Sheila lays her head on his shoulder and James lays his head on hers. They continue to glide across the floor and he dips Sheila to her surprise. All of sudden they come to a stop. James's expression on his face changes quickly. Sheila looks up to see a stunning, tall woman standing over them. "Lauren, what are you doing here?"

"I'm in town for business. I thought I would come by and say hi. I'm sorry about Ms. La Rue." James remembers he has Sheila in her arms and lifts her back up. She's just happy he didn't drop her.

"This is Ms. Sheila Jones. She's the new owner. And this is Ms. Lauren Grant. She's an old friend."

"We were a little more than that I think. I see you haven't lost your moves." Ms. Grant has all her attention focused on James. It's almost like Sheila doesn't even exist.

"Nice to meet you, Ms. Grant. I'll let you guys catch up." They talk for a few moments and make plans to have lunch soon. They hug each other goodbye. James and Sheila continue to work in silence. Sheila is curious about Lauren. It seems like there was more than friendship between them and the look on his face when she walked in the door suggests that as well. But it's not any of her business. James seems different and more quiet than usual.

Their parents and Samantha finally come back with a pizza in their hands and ice cream. "We're back!" Sheila's mom feels like something's not right.

"Mom, it took you that long to get a pizza?"

"There was a lot of traffic and people in the restaurant."

"No there wasn't. You and Grandpa said we should take our time so you guys could spend some time alone together." Her grandpa gives her a look. "Sorry, Grandpa!" Everyone starts laughing. The two of them stop painting and eat. Sheila thanks everyone for their help. She wants to show her gratitude by cooking dinner for them. James tells her she doesn't have to do that. It'll be too much trouble and work. But Sheila wants to and insists that it would be no trouble at all, and her mom would love having them. His dad and Samantha would love to come over for dinner. His dad really wants to see the garden. James is outvoted. They make plans for dinner and finish up the painting.

The next day Sheila and her mom are working in the yard. Sheila's mom asks her what happened when they left to get lunch. Sheila tells her about Lauren. "You don't believe they're just friends?" Her mom hands Sheila a flower.

"Yes. I don't know. She didn't act like it and she wasn't shy about it either." She puts the flower in the hole and presses it down in the ground with her feet. She starts digging another hole.

"James said they're old friends and I think you should believe him. You said you weren't interested in him anyway." Sheila's mom hands her another flower.

"I'm not. I have my classes, the gallery, and the estate to worry about and you."

"I told you about worrying about me."

"As long as you're my mama I'm going to worry about you."

"And as long as you're my baby I'm going to worry about you." They finish up planting the rest of the flowers and start cooking dinner. After dinner Sheila does some studying and homework. It's been a while since she Skyped with Eliza. It's late so she decides to wait and Skype with her tomorrow. The next day she Skypes with Eliza. They get caught up. Sheila talks about the gallery, the business and art classes, and mentions James. Eliza can tell she's excited and she seems happy. Eliza wants to know when the grand opening is. Sheila promises she'll let her know so Eliza and her family can come down for it and visit.

Chapter 16

The day for James and his family to come over for dinner has come. Sheila and her mom straighten up and clean the house from top to bottom. Sheila doesn't seem nervous to her mom's surprise. She seems fairly at ease. But as the arrival time approaches her mom detects some excitement. She helps Sheila in the kitchen with the appetizers. When they finish the appetizers they start preparing dinner. Her mom looks up at the clock. "Sheila, shouldn't you be getting ready?"

"I thought I was ready."

"I think you should wear that red dress you just bought. It looks so stunning on you."

"Mom, it's just James."

"Please, for me. You don't have to wait for a special occasion to wear nice clothes."

"Okay, Mom!" Sheila runs to change into the dress.

Just as she finishes dressing and doing her hair the doorbell rings. Her mom opens it. "Hi, guys! Come in and make yourselves at home. You look cute, Samantha."

"Thank you, Mrs. Jones. Where's Ms. Sheila?"

"She'll be out in a minute."

"My dad made a coconut cream pie for dessert."

"You didn't have to, but thank you. It looks good." As they make themselves comfortable Sheila's mom offers them the appetizers and something to drink. James's dad comments on how beautiful the flowers are and the home as well. Sheila appears from around the corner and all eyes are on her. James and his dad standup.

"You look real pretty, Ms. Sheila."

Then James's dad bumps James's arm. "I think so too."

"Thank you. Dinner should be ready in about an hour." Sheila's mom shows James's dad the plants in the back.

James offers his help in the kitchen and Sheila begins to laugh. "Do you think you can handle setting the table?"

"Yes, I think I can do that."

"And Ms. Samantha I think you can help me in the kitchen."

"Yes, ma'am!"

While Sheila's mom is showing James's dad the backyard she takes the opportunity to ask about Lauren. They met in college their freshmen year. It became quite serious. When they graduated she got a job fairly quickly and he had trouble. Then his mom became sick. As the disease progressed his mother needed twenty-four-hour care and supervision. He put job hunting on the backburner to help his dad care for his mom. His sister did what she could but she had her own family. Lauren was doing well at her job. They were spending less time together and she didn't feel comfortable spending time at their home. She urged him to go back to job hunting, and she thought they should put his mom in a home. His dad was not going to do that and James supported his decision. Eventually they broke up, but stayed friends. After his mom passed away he got a job as an accountant, but he tried to get one in architecture. No one seemed to be impressed with his designs. He makes good money as an accountant, but he misses designing. Lauren and James decided to get back together. He was seriously considering marrying her, and then his sister and brother-in-law died in the car accident. James decided it would be best if he raised Samantha and his sister put in the will that he was to become her legal guardian if anything happened to them. Lauren thought James should sign guardianship over to his father but he didn't. He thought it would be best if he took responsibility for her and his dad helped him. Lauren got promoted, but she would have to move to New York. James wasn't going to uproot Samantha and take her away from her grandpa and everything she knew. She was still dealing with her parents' death. They decided to break it off. His dad is hoping that they do not start back up again. As James's dad is talking Sheila's mom remembers when her husband was sick. She couldn't have taken care of him or gotten through it without Sheila's help, and she feels the same way about Linda when she got sick and passed away. She thanks God just about every day for Sheila. "Lauren's timing couldn't be better."

"You're right. She drops back into his life just when he comes into his inheritance."

Samantha comes running outside. "Dinner is ready."

"We're coming, bunny." As they're coming in Sheila and James are putting the food on the table.

Sheila is surprised by a big hug from her mom. "What was that for?"

"For just being you. I love you, pumpkin."

"I love you too, mom." James's dad blesses the food. As they eat they talk about flowers, the gallery, and how Sheila's classes are going. She wants to put in wood flooring. She's not sure if she wants to install it herself or hire someone to do it. James offers his help. He helped his dad put wood flooring in the kitchen and put wood flooring in Ms. La Rue's home. Sheila takes him up on the offer. After James and his family thank them for a delicious dinner and leave, Sheila and her mom clear the table and clean up the kitchen. guardianship over to his father but he didn't. He thought it would be best if he took responsibility for her and his dad helped him. Lauren got promoted, but she would have to move to New York. James wasn't going to uproot Samantha and take her away from her grandpa and everything she knew. She was still dealing with her parents' death. They decided to break it off. His dad is hoping that they do not start back up again. As James's dad is talking Sheila's mom remembers when her husband was sick. She couldn't have taken care of him or gotten through it without Sheila's help, and she feels the same way about Linda when she got sick and passed away. She thanks God just about every day for Sheila. "Lauren's timing couldn't be better."

"You're right. She drops back into his life just when he comes into his inheritance."

Samantha comes running outside. "Dinner is ready."

"We're coming, bunny." As they're coming in Sheila and James are putting the food on the table.

Sheila is surprised by a big hug from her mom. "What was that for?"

"For just being you. I love you, pumpkin."

"I love you too, mom." James's dad blesses the food. As they eat they talk about flowers, the gallery, and how Sheila's classes are going. She wants to put in wood flooring. She's not sure if she wants to install it herself or hire someone to do it. James offers his help. He helped his dad put wood flooring in the kitchen and put wood flooring in Ms. La Rue's home. Sheila takes him up on the offer. After James and his family thank them for a delicious dinner and leave, Sheila and her mom clear the table and clean up the kitchen.

Chapter 17

A week later James and Sheila go to Home Depot to pick out wood flooring. Her mom decides to tag along to be nosey about the flowers. While her mom is looking at the flowers James and Sheila are inside looking at the different hues of wood. James likes this one but she thinks it's too dark. Sheila sees another one that she likes, but James thinks it's too light. She spots another one that could be perfect. It's dark enough, but it's not too light. They agree on that one. Another shopper comments on their choice. "I like the one you two picked out. What room in the house are the two of you doing?"

Sheila looks at the woman strangely. "It's not for the house. It's for my new business."

"You're not married? Sorry, but you two make such a cute couple."

Now James is looking strange. "That's okay, ma'am. Have a nice day."

"You too." James grabs a few tools and supplies they might need. After Sheila pays for everything they look for her mom. When they find her she wants to look around some more. James offers to take Sheila home after they do some work at the gallery. James loads up his truck and they head for the gallery.

Sheila notices a nice swing in the truck bed. "Did you build that? It's beautiful."

"Thank you. It's a surprise for a friend." When they arrive at the gallery James hands Sheila a pair of gloves. They start unloading the truck. Once they're finished James starts pulling up the old floor. As he's pulling it up Sheila takes it to the dumpster. Once all of it is up and the space is cleared and cleaned they start laying the wood flooring. Sheila needs some music so she turns the CD player on. Once most of the wood flooring is laid they decide to take a break and eat. "Where do you want to go to eat?"

"Here." Sheila looks oddly at James. "Wait a minute!" James rushes out and a few moments later he returns with a picnic basket and a blanket in his arms. He spreads the blanket out and sets the floor. As they sit down Sheila can't believe he did all this. He takes out salad, lasagna, strawberry shortcake, and sweet tea.

"You put this together?"

"Honestly no. My dad made the lasagna, but I made the salad, the dessert, and the tea."

"So you did all the hard stuff?"

"Exactly." They both start laughing.

Sheila takes a few bites of the lasagna and a couple swallows of the tea. "This is good. James, why are you doing this?"

"Doing what?"

"Helping me with the gallery and everything."

"Because I hope we're friends. I think you have become a really good friend."

"I consider you a good friend as well. Have you given the estate any thought?"

"You might be right about not selling it. My sister and I spent quite a bit of time there. I have quite a few good and happy memories of the place."

"It might take me some time to buy you out."

"Maybe we could share it. I'm sure we could figure out a way to make it work. We better finish eating before the food gets cold." When they get to dessert Sheila takes one bite and feels like she's in heaven. James hears the song they danced to last time. He stands up and holds out his hand. "May I have this dance? I believe this is our song." Sheila takes his hand. He pulls her up and close to him. They start moving across the wood flooring that they put in so far. "I think the floor is looking nice. We did a pretty good job so far."

"You can dance, put in flooring, and design. What can't you do?"

"I can't cook. You forgot that fact?" Sheila starts laughing. James thinks to himself, She has such a warm and beautiful smile. Then he twirls her and pulls her in close. They start swaying from side to side with Sheila's head on his chest.

Life's Unexpected Blessings

A few moments later James's dad and Samantha appear in the doorway. "The floor is looking real nice. You got quite a bit done too."

The two of them are caught by surprise and stop dancing instantly. "How long have you been standing there?"

"Not for very long. And I taught him those moves."

Sheila and James start laughing again. "I think it was more like mom taught me those moves." Then his dad starts to laugh. His dad helps them finish laying the wood flooring. Sheila thanks his dad for the lasagna.

She locks up the gallery and James and Samantha take her home with his dad following. "Why is your dad following us?

"So he can help me deliver the swing to my friend." When they arrive at Sheila's home James and his dad unload the swing. "Where do you want the swing?"

Sheila has a stunned look on her face. Then her mom comes out with a surprised look on her face. "I'm the friend you wanted to surprise with the swing?"

"Yes! And mission accomplished."

"Mom, where should we put it?"

"I think it would look good in the back. It's beautiful." They take it to the back and sit it in the middle of the yard between two plants. Sheila, James, and Samantha try it out. "We'll see you back at the house."

"Sure, Dad."

"Bye, Sheila!"

"Bye, Mr. Logan!" Samantha gives both Sheila and James a hug and kiss. Sheila's mom walks them out.

"I finished the benches and made a sketch for the metal gazebo." James pulls out his leather notebook and shows Sheila.

"I love it! It's really good."

"I also sketched a children's table and chairs. I know you wanted to make the gallery more inviting to kids."

"This is really good too. It's fun and whimsical." As he's showing her the sketches and talking Sheila notices a change in him. He just lights up. "Do you miss this?"

"Sometimes. Why?"

"You're really good at this and you seem to really enjoy it."

"My job as an accountant pays well and helps me take care of Samantha. And it helps my dad out too. But I do receive more joy from designing and working with my hands."

"Have you ever thought about getting back into it?"

"I don't know. After I graduated college I tried to get a job in architecture. I guess nobody liked my designs. My accountant job is a sure thing and the hours are flexible. And I have Samantha to think about."

"Why not do it on the side or even start your own business? Submit or get your designs out there. There has to be somebody who would be interested."

"It's something to think about. Do you miss studying medicine?"

"Not as much as I thought I would. When I reopen the gallery and get it established and finish my business degree I might become an RN. I still have my school books that I look through on occasion and refer to. But my passion and joy resides in art."

"You're a very a talented artist and your passion comes through in your art. I think you would have made a wonderful doctor or nurse. There's nothing I can't see you doing and not succeeding at. Oh, how are your business classes going?"

"Pretty good, but there are a few things I'm having trouble with." Sheila goes inside to get her school stuff and show it to James. He explains it to her and it makes perfect sense. Sheila hears her mom's voice and looks up to see her standing on the porch with the phone in her hand.

"It's Jason."

"O.k. I'll be there in a few."

James looks down at his watch and didn't realize how late it was. "I better go before they send a search party for me."

"Thanks for your help."

"Sure, no problem." As James walks off his cell phone rings. He answers it. "I'm on my way home right now."

Chapter 18

Sheila is tired and sore from helping James with the floor, but things still need to get done around the house. The gutters and flower beds need cleaning out and her mom wants to rearrange some flower pots in the front. Sheila doesn't like being still. She likes staying busy. Sheila meets with her study group later that day at the library. They have a big exam coming up in a couple days. She explains to them what James explained to her. It helps them quite a bit. As the study group is leaving Jason and Sheila walk together. "Are you nervous about the exam?"

"I was, but not so much. Hey, you want to get a cup of coffee? I know a great place really close by."

Sheila gives it some thought. "Okay. But it has to be short. I need to get home." Jason is happy with any time he can spend with her. He's been wanting to ask her out for weeks and he has finally worked up the courage to do so. Sheila follows him in her car. When they arrive at the coffee shop they talk about the class and the teacher. They're both glad the class will be over with very soon. They talk about the other classes they'll be taking. Sheila cuts it short. "Jason, I have to go. It was nice having coffee with you and chatting."

"Maybe we could do it again."

"Maybe. Bye!"

James calls to let Sheila know he's finished the benches, children furniture, and metal gazebo. The next day Sheila and her mom meet James at the gallery. They start unloading his truck. When they step inside Sheila's mom can't believe they put this floor in. She thinks the two of them did a beautiful job on it. The first thing Sheila does is put music on. As Sheila and her mom are arranging the furniture and grooving to the music James is putting the gazebo together. He looks up and starts grinning.

"What are you laughing at?"

"Nothing. I'm just admiring your moves." Sheila lets out a laugh. "I need someone to watch Samantha this evening. My dad is busy. She's been wanting to spend some time with you."

"Sure. Could you drop her off at the estate? Mom and I are going over there after we finish up here. I saw some furniture that might look nice in here."

"Okay. That's fine."

Sheila and her mom pick up a few items from the grocery store on the way to the estate. They'll have dinner there probably. A few moments later James pulls up with Samantha. She runs straight to Sheila and gives her a big hug.

"You look very handsome this evening. You got a hot date?"

"Thank you and no. Just having dinner with Lauren before she goes back to New York. Samantha, be good. She has some homework."

"Okay. If you want my mom and I can take her home."

"That would be great. My dad should be home around seven o'clock. Here's my cell and home number. Call me if there's any problem."

Samantha gives her uncle a hug and runs in the house. Sheila waves goodbye. Samantha sits down at the kitchen table and pulls out her homework and a sketch book.

"May I look at your sketch book?"

"Sure. I thought we could do some sketching together."

"Okay. But first you have to do your homework. Then we can do some sketching after dinner. I'll be right here. If you need help just let me know." While Sheila's starting dinner her mom is looking around the house for furniture that would look nice in the gallery. She finds a few items that she shows Sheila. Samantha yells for Sheila. She's having trouble with a math problem so Sheila helps her. Sheila checks on the food in the kitchen. Samantha starts her English homework which is her worst subject. Sheila sits beside her and has her read aloud at her own speed. English wasn't Sheila's favorite subject either. She didn't like it when the teacher would make her stand up in front of the other kids and read out loud. Sheila looks over her homework. It looks good to her. Sheila fixes everyone's plates and blesses the food. After they finish dinner they go in the backyard. On the way outside Sheila notices some paintings in the corner and pauses.

"My mom painted those. She was an artist."

Sheila takes a closer look at them. "They're beautiful." Sheila sees a picture of a couple holding a small child. She picks up the framed picture. "Is that you and your parents?"

Samantha gets this sad look on her face. "Yes. My uncle told me I was one or two. Ms. Sheila do you miss your dad?"

"At first I missed him just about every day and I had to get used to him not being there. But as time went by I missed him less. I will always love him and miss him just like you will always love and miss your mom. They're still here in our hearts."

"My mom was fun, funny, nice, and pretty like you."

"You look just like her. You have her eyes and smile." Sheila gives her a big hug. "I thought you wanted to sketch!"

Samantha's face lights up. "Yeah!" They continue outside where she shows Sheila and her mom the sketches. For a child her age they're very good. She talks about how she and her mom would sketch together.

James wonders what Sheila and Samantha are doing right now. He would rather be with them instead of here. Lauren made the reservations at this very fancy and nice restaurant. As Lauren is talking she feels as though James is not listening. He seems like he's somewhere else. "James, are you here?"

"What? Oh, sorry. I just hope Samantha is okay."

"I'm sure she's fine. You can call your dad to make sure."

"She's with Ms. Jones. My dad was busy this evening."

Lauren is surprised. "Are you and Ms. Jones an item?"

"No. She's just a good friend. Lauren, why did you bring me here?"

"Do you miss me? I miss you. Have you thought about what could have been?"

"You live in New York and I live here."

"What if there was a fantastic job opportunity there for you?"

"What are you talking about?"

"I gave your resume to my boss. And he wants to hire you. He'll pay your expenses to relocate. The money you got from Ms. La Rue's will would help you get settled."

"Wait! I didn't tell you about Ms. La Rue's will. And I can't just uproot Samantha."

"Your dad could take her. I'm sure you could get quite a bit of money for Ms. La Rue's estate."

"I love Samantha like she's my own child and the estate belongs to me and Sheila. We're not selling it."

"What are you and her going to do with it?"

"None of your concern. And I lost my appetite." James calls the waiter over and asks for the check. They leave.

When James comes home he finds his dad sitting on the couch. "I'm assuming things went badly with Lauren."

"You could say that. I'm going to go tell Samantha goodnight."

"She's not home yet. Sheila called. She wasn't ready to come home yet. But they'll be here soon." James sits down on the couch next to his dad. "What happened with Lauren?"

"She found out about the will and there's a great job opportunity in New York for me. And it's mine if I want it."

"What did you tell her?"

"All the reasons why I'm not taking it. And she asked about Sheila."

"And what did you say about her?"

"That we're good friends."

"Are you sure about that? You can deny it all you want, but I've seen you two together. There's a spark. Maybe you should explore it. Sheila is a strong, smart, beautiful inside and out, and kind woman. And Samantha likes her very much. It's only a matter of time before someone scoops her up."

His dad has a point and James thinks he might be too late. "I saw her having coffee with this guy yesterday."

"Well, did you say hi to her?"

"No, I didn't. I didn't want to intrude. She didn't see me anyway."

"So, you don't know who he was?" The doorbell rings. His dad gets up to answer it. "You finally decided to come home. I thought you ran away."

Samantha laughs. "No, Grandpa. I would miss you."

"Your flowers are beautiful."

"Thank you. There's a lot more in the back yard."

"Sheila, I'll just be a few moments." Sheila sits down on the couch beside James and Samantha.

"Did you and Ms. Sheila have fun?"

"Yes! We sketched and ate dinner." She shows her uncle some of the sketches.

"What about your homework?"

"I did it and Ms. Sheila helped me."

"Okay. Get ready for bed and brush your teeth."

Samantha jumps up and turns to Ms. Sheila. "You'll say bye before you go?" Sheila nods yes. She scampers off with a smile on her face.

"Thank you for watching her."

"It was my pleasure. Are you okay?"

"Yeah. I just have a lot on my mind."

"Anything I can help you with?"

"No. I'll be fine. So, I'm guessing you'll be reopening the gallery soon. Are you going to rename it?"

"I was thinking about naming it The Soulful Art Gallery. I saw your sister's paintings. They're very good. I was thinking about putting them up in the gallery. If I sold any of them all the money would go to you. I wouldn't even take commission."

"One of her paintings was already hung up in the gallery."

"Which one?"

"The one with the two children at the beach making a sand castle. That was us."

Now Sheila understands why he was looking at that painting all the time. "Or you can just take the paintings. They rightfully belong to your family. Actually you can have anything you want. You don't mind if I use some of the furniture?"

"No. I'll think about my sister's paintings. Do you have a date in mind for the reopening?"

"I'm thinking in two weeks. I'm going to put an ad in the newspaper and make some flyers to pass out."

Her mom comes in from the back porch. "Sheila, you should see the flowers in the back. You ready to go?"

"I have to say bye to Samantha first."

Chapter 19

A few days later Sheila makes up the flyers and calls up the newspaper. She also calls up the contacts she made at her art show. She has kept in contact with the artists that Ms. La Rue showed in the gallery. She has been letting the artists know the progress of the gallery, and she would like to continue showing their art if she has their permission. Sheila will keep the same agreement that the artists had with Ms. La Rue. She hopes they will and after some thought they say yes. Sheila and her mom decide to take a walk around the neighborhood and pass out some fliers. "So, are you nervous?"

"A little. What if this is a bust?"

"Well, you have nothing to lose. You can still do your art and show it in another gallery. Or go back into medicine. You have options."

"My mom is such a wise lady. But she needs to give herself more credit."

"I have a wonderful smart daughter who needs to believe in herself."

"I wish Dad was here to see this and Linda too."

"Me too." They give each other a big hug. As they reach the house James and Samantha drive up. James gets out but Samantha stays in the car waving with a big smile on her face. He can't stay. He just came by to pick up some fliers to pass out. Sheila appreciates that a lot.

The next day she picks up Eliza and her family from the airport. When Sheila arrives at the airport she finds them standing by the baggage claim. "Hey, lady!"

"Hey yourself!" Sheila and Eliza are so happy to see each other that they can't contain there excitement.

"Do you have everything?"

"We're still waiting for one or two bags." Once they have all their luggage they head to Sheila's home. While they're getting settled Sheila and her mom make dinner. As they're eating dinner they all catch up. After dinner Sheila and Eliza go outside and sit on the swing. They talk and reminisce about the old days. They talk about the gallery and other things. "So, James built and designed this swing for you?"

"Yes. Isn't it beautiful?"

"Very! So tell me about James."

"Nothing to tell. He's a good friend, good guy, smart, and good with his hands."

"Are you sure about just being good friends? Would a friend do this?"

"Yes. And how's the program going?"

"Good. I finished it a couple weeks ago. When do I get to meet him?"

"Tomorrow if you want to help finish setting up the gallery."

After a good night's sleep they meet James and his family at the estate. Sheila makes the introductions. Sheila points out the pieces she's going to use in the gallery. James, his dad, and Eliza's husband load up the truck. "May I take these pictures and that painting?"

"Sure, Mr. Logan. I told your son that you were welcome to anything in the house you wanted."

"Thank you." Once they're finished loading the furniture and rounding up the kids they head to the gallery.

When they arrive Sheila shows Eliza around. Then they start positioning the furniture and re-hanging the paintings. When they're done everybody stands back and takes a good look. "The gallery looks really nice."

"It'll look even better once I add my mom's flowers."

"And I have some you can add to them."

"Are you sure, Mr. Logan? You don't have to."

"I want to. Well, I'm hungry. Anybody else?" They all decide to go out to dinner.

Eliza's kids have been bugging her to take them to Disneyland. She gives in and plans on taking them tomorrow. "Can Auntie Sheila and Samantha come with us?"

"Sure. You guys want to come?"

"Uncle James, can I?"

"If it's not an intrusion that's fine."

"James, why don't you come too?"

Eliza likes that idea. Then she could get to know James better. "That's a good idea. You and Sheila have been working so hard on the gallery. Both of you need to have some fun and relax. Afterwards we can have dinner celebrating the reopening of the gallery at Sheila's and James's house." Everyone is looking confused and a little stunned. "The estate the two of them inherited." Then the confused and stunned looks disappear.

The next day James and Samantha meet them at Sheila's home. Eliza suggests that she, James, and Sheila ride together while the kids ride with her husband. This way she'll have a chance to grill James. When they arrive they decide to split up and meet back there at one o'clock. The boys go one way and the girls go the other way. Before they know it it's time to meet back up. After all that walking and getting on rides they're hungry. They decide to have lunch at one of the restaurants in the park. James orders for Samantha, Sheila, and himself. Eliza's husband orders for his family. As they wait for the food the kids talk about the rides and the park and all the Disney characters they saw. When the food arrives the kids dive right in. This gives Eliza a chance to grill James some more. "So, James do you have a girlfriend or someone special?" Sheila hits her arm and gives Eliza a look.

"No. It's just me and Samantha. We like it that way."

"That's right, but I like it too when it's me, Sheila and you."

"Is there someone you're interested in, James?"

"No not really."

"I thought you like Sheila, Uncle James."

"I do, but she's a very good friend."

"I don't get adults."

James is starting to become uncomfortable, so he changes the subject quickly. "So what was Sheila like in college?"

"You're going to tell that story?" Eliza has all of James's attention. Eliza's husband heard the story countless times before so he continues to eat.

"There's a story? This should be interesting."

Sheila sits there preparing herself for the words that are about to come out of Eliza mouth. "We both were accepted early admission and in this program that required the students to arrive early for orientation. After the parents got their kids setup in their dorm rooms and left, all the students went down to the common area to mingle." This is the part of the story that

Sheila does not like. "I saw this shy, quiet girl sitting in the corner looking pitiful and sad all by herself."

"I was not looking pitiful and sad. I was in a room full of strangers. This was totally new to me and I was missing my parents."

"May I continue?"

"Yes, but I will correct you as you go."

"Fine. So I went up to her and started talking. From that day on we became the best of friends. We hung out and did everything together just about. When our family came into town to visit, all of us went out to dinner together. We majored in the same thing, but I couldn't hang in there. Pre-med was too tough for me so I changed my major to English. We were roommates for almost four and a half years."

"I remember the first apartment we rented. My dad helped me find it."

"I thought you guys were living in a dorm?"

"Sheila, you want to explain that one?"

"Well, I didn't fill in the dorm room application because I didn't know anyone going to UF. It didn't matter to me who I got for a roommate. I thought I should be able to get along with anyone. I guess the person assigned to me thought different. She knew the person in mind that she wanted as a roommate and it wasn't me. After a week or two of living together she talked me into switching rooms with the girl she wanted as a roommate. They literally moved my stuff the next day. And I almost got in trouble for it because there are steps or procedures that need to be followed when changing roommates. Apparently all she cared about was having her friend as a roommate."

"She sounds pretty bad and used to getting what she wants."

"Well it worked out for the best because her friend's roommate was a better match and became one of our good friends."

"Sheila and I didn't like living in the dorm so she suggested we rent an apartment together. I had my doubts because I wasn't used to living with girls. I didn't have any sisters, but only brothers."

"But I knew. I had a good feeling about it."

"She was right. We had fun and a lot of laughs while we were getting our education of course. I found out Sheila wasn't as shy or quiet as I thought and she's crazy and funny without knowing it."

"You're crazy too! That's why we're such good friends."

Eliza's husband stops eating to put his two cents in. "She's right. My wife is crazy." They start laughing.

"I also found out she's an honest, nice, sweet person."

"You're not too bad yourself." Sheila and Eliza give each other a hug.

"So you guys were perfect strangers until the first day of college? It's almost like you were both meant to attend UF and become friends. It's like God had a hand in it."

Sheila never looked at it that way. "I don't know, but I'm glad she was there. She watched out for me and I hope I watched out for her. I think we grew up a little." After they finish up lunch they head back to Sheila's home.

As Sheila's mom is looking out the kitchen window she sees their car pull up into the driveway and meets them at the front door. "Did you guys have fun?" The kids are laughing, smiling, and jumping around.

"I think we did. What have you been up to?"

"I was getting the plants together and made a pound cake for dessert."

"We were thinking about spending the night at the estate."

"That's not a bad idea. It might be too late to drive back home and in the morning we can head straight over to the gallery."

"The kids are definitely for it. They're calling it a slumber party." Everybody packs an overnight bag. They load the cars up with the plants and head over to James's home.

While Sheila is helping Samantha pack an overnight bag he calls his dad. "I told my dad about spending the night at the estate. He thinks it's a good idea. Your mom, Eliza, the children, and you can go ahead. We'll meet you guys over there. My dad wants me to gather some stuff. I'll see if Eliza's husband will help me."

"Okay. I'll tell them."

When they arrive at the estate they notice a countertop full of groceries. The kids immediately drop their bags by the door and run straight to the backyard to play. James's dad comes from the back. "So how was Disneyland?"

"It was fun but I had my fill of it for a while."

"I agree."

"I'm grilling the meat in the back. I thought you guys could prepare the sides. Whatever you come up with is fine." Sheila, her mom, and Eliza look through the groceries and come up with a menu that includes deviled eggs, stuffed mushrooms, garden salad, mac and cheese, corn on the cob, and collard greens. Sheila is eager to show Eliza around the house. During the tour they find an old record player and a collection of vinyl records. They pick a few out and start playing them.

"This house is beautiful! And you and James are going to share it?"

"We decided not to sell it and co-own it for now. We haven't worked out all the details."

"You guys are just friends?"

"We should go help my mom." They're in the kitchen cooking and grooving to the music.

Soon the guys show up. "Where's the party at?"

"Right here!" They all start laughing. "The kids are in the back playing and your dad's back there grilling the meat."

"Do you guys need some help?"

"No. We got it under control."

"Okay. I'll go help my dad. Michael, you want to come help too?"

"That sounds like a good idea. I hate to leave the party, ladies. Try not to miss us too much."

"We'll try not to. My husband the comedian." They laugh. Once they get most of the sides prepared Sheila and Eliza plop down on the couch. It's been a long, but enjoyable day. They will definitely sleep well tonight. Sheila's mom goes out to the garden.

"I bet your mom has fun in that garden."

"Yes, she does. It's like her own playground."

"Now back to you and James."

"There is no me and James. We're just friends and that's it. I need to focus on the gallery anyway."

Suddenly Eliza's husband, Michael, appears from the back. "James thinks of you as more than just a friend."

"How do you know?"

"All he did was talk about you and asked a lot of questions concerning you. He looks at you like he's falling for you but doesn't know it yet. He's cool and a good guy."

"What did you say?"

"That you are cool and crazy."

"Michael, don't mess with her."

"I meant the good crazy. I also said you're a strong willed, opinionated, smart and good woman. Sweet too. I think he's just scared. Lauren did a number on him."

Eliza gets this curious look on her face. "Whose Lauren?"

"She's his ex-girlfriend. They have remained friends over the years and still are."

All of a sudden the kids rush through the back door. "Hey! You guys need to calm down. Remember you're a guest in someone else's home. Be respectful."

"Yes, sir."

Michael whispers in Eliza's ear. "There's more. He almost proposed to her."

"Do not mention that to Sheila."

"Okay. I know it's not my place to say anything."

Samantha plops down next to Sheila. "Grandpa says the meat will be ready in about an hour."

"Okay. Will you please take the corn on the cob out to him? Then you can come back and help me set the table."

"Yes ma'am."

"Thank you." After they set the table Eliza and Michael also help Sheila hang some paintings.

"What were the two of you whispering about?"

Eliza just remembered Sheila notices everything. "Just wife and husband stuff." Then they figure out the sleeping arrangements. When the meat is done James and his dad bring it in and sit it on the table with the rest of the food. The spread on the table looks beautiful and they can't wait to dig in. James's dad blesses the food.

"Before we dig in I would like to thank everyone for their help. Mom, thank you for your support. It means the world to me. Eliza, I want to thank you and your family for coming down. I especially want to thank James and his family for all their help." Sheila focuses her attention directly on James. "You went above and beyond. Okay. Everybody, dig in!"

James notices that something is different about the room. "You put my sister's paintings up."

"I thought when you or your dad or Samantha are here it'll be like your sister is here too. A pleasant reminder I guess you can say. I hope that was okay." James doesn't know what to say. After dinner James and Michael clear the table and wash the dishes while his dad and Sheila's mom put the food up. Eliza and Sheila are getting the kids ready for bed. Once their heads hit the pillows they fall straight off to sleep. Sheila's excitement and nerves keep her awake, however, so she decides to get a snack out of the kitchen. She thinks there's some sweet potato pie left. She approaches the kitchen table to see that James has the same idea.

He looks up to his surprise to see Sheila standing there. "I guess I wasn't the only one having trouble sleeping." James stands up and pulls a chair out for her. "Won't you join me in a slice of pie?"

Sheila sits down while James cuts her a slice. "Thank you."

"What's your excuse for being up so late?"

Sheila takes a bite. "Excitement and nervousness. More nervousness than excitement. What's your excuse?"

"I was just looking at my sister's paintings. There are some good memories there. Especially the one of us at the beach. It reminds me of simpler, less complicated times."

"Well, I felt that one belonged here. And I understand longing for those days. When you decide to become a caregiver or help care for someone you truly do not know what that means or involves until you do it. Then becoming a dad instantly."

"I wasn't prepared for my mom getting sick. But I definitely wasn't prepared to become a dad instantly."

"Well, you are doing a great job with her. At least you got to skip potty training."

James lets out a big chuckle. "Well, thank you. But I still have to get through the teenage years which scare me to death."

"Just keep doing what you're doing. Hopefully she'll feel comfortable and trust you enough to come to you when she needs to talk. Just make sure you listen."

"My sister would have liked you a lot. You guys would have been best friends. She was funny and she could make me laugh like nobody. She would have told you all my secrets."

"I have none and don't you dare think about going to Eliza."

"If you have no secrets you shouldn't be worried about me going to Eliza." James laughs a bit.

"You don't mention your sister much. What was she like?"

"My sister and I had a complicated relationship. I loved her and she loved me. She was several years older than me, nine years to be exact. She didn't have it easy. But I felt like the oldest and people who met us would think that. She was bipolar and mildly schizophrenic which was diagnosed and treated late in her life. Then she had problems with her intestines and kidneys. I wouldn't say she was dumb or mentally retarded, but maybe mildly slow."

James notices the time on the clock in the kitchen. "I get the feeling you were a good sister. Oh, we've been talking for quite a while. You need to get your sleep. You have nothing to be nervous about tomorrow. You will be fine and do great."

Talking with James actually eased her nervousness. "You're right." Both James and Sheila go to their rooms to try to get some sleep. Before they know it it's time to get up and get everybody together. While the girls and the boys are getting themselves together James's dad is cooking some breakfast. Everybody eats quickly.

On the way out the door Sheila stops and looks at Ms. La Rue's urn sitting on the fireplace mantle. "I hope you knew what you were doing."

"Sheila, come on! You don't want to be late for your own reopening."

"I'm coming, Mom." When they arrive at the gallery Sheila stands in the center of the room taking everything in for a few moments. Then she gets to work. First they arrange the plants in the metal gazebo. Then they arrange the bouquets of flowers that are situated throughout the gallery for décor. They hang the rest of the paintings. James's dad hands each woman and young lady a single yellow rose. As James is pinning Sheila's yellow rose she notices a beautiful wrapped package under his arm.

When he's finished he hands her the package. "This is for you. I hope you like it." Sheila opens it very careful. It's a beautiful, carved, wooden sign that reads "The Soulful Art Gallery".

"Thank you. I love it!"

"Well, put it up." Sheila decides to hang it in the window. As she's positioning and hanging it a familiar face appears. It's Lauren. James is surprised and annoyed to see her.

"Ms. Grant, nice to see you again."

"Ms. Jones, much improvement since the last time I saw it." James and Lauren step outside to talk.

Everyone is acting like they're busy but are actually watching them. Especially her mom and Eliza. "Is that Lauren?"

"Yes."

"She's not that pretty and she comes off very cold."

"She has chicken legs."

"She's snooty too. That's what my grandpa says."

"You guys ought to be ashamed of yourselves. You're not setting a very good example. We need to get this place together. I'm opening the doors in ten minutes." Sheila's right, but they're more interested in what's happening outside. They're working and watching at the same time.

"Lauren, what are you doing here? I thought you were back in New York."

"Did you give anymore thought to our discussion during dinner?"

"The answer is still no. And by the way I didn't miss you one bit." He turns and walks away.

Lauren crosses her arms and a stern look comes across her face. "No one turns their back on me. Do you know what you're doing?"

"Yes, I do. I actually feel sorry for you. You haven't changed at all. The next time you're in town don't bother stopping by to say hi." Lauren storms off. When James walks back in everyone turns their attention away from the door quickly. James stands there for a moment looking at Sheila. He thinks to himself that it might be time to take a leap of faith. It might be different with Sheila. He takes a deep breath and starts walking towards Sheila. She's making flower arrangements with her mom and Eliza. James softly touches her shoulder. She turns around to see that it's James. He looks strange.

"Are you okay?"

"Oh, I'm fine. But Sheila, can we talk?"

Sheila looks at her mom and Eliza. "We can finish this. You and James go talk."

"Okay. We can talk in the office, I guess."

As they walk into the office James closes the door and turns on the music. "I believe our song is playing. May I have this dance?" He holds out his hand for Sheila to take. He pulls her in close and they start dancing.

"How come we always end up dancing? And I thought you wanted to talk."

"I just want to see if we'll ever get to finish a dance. And we're talking. If I haven't mentioned it yet you look beautiful."

"Thank you. And where's Lauren?"

"On her way back to New York. I'm pretty sure I won't be seeing her any time soon. Is your boyfriend coming?"

"Boyfriend?"

"The man you were having coffee with."

"Oh! He's a classmate of mine. I didn't see you at the coffee shop."

James is relieved to hear that. "I didn't want to intrude. Isn't it funny how our lives took such different paths than what we planned or expected?"

"And how those paths came together? Maybe this is the path we're meant to be on or follow."

"Maybe we're meant to be on or follow this path together."

They hear a knock at the door, and it's Eliza. She's not surprised to see Sheila in James's arms. "Sorry, but I think you better get out here. Quite a few people are starting to come in."

"I guess we'll never get to finish our dance."

"There's always hope." They step out of the office and Sheila is surprised and amazed by the number of people in the gallery. She thinks to herself, This might actually work. James gently but firmly grasps her hand and he pulls her close. "Will you do me the honor of going out on a date with me? Just you and me."

"I would love to." Then their faces come in close and they kiss. Sheila doesn't know what the future holds, and she admits that's scary, but she knows tomorrow is not promised. As she looks around the room she sees her mom, Eliza and her family, James's dad, and Samantha laughing and smiling. Sheila decides she is going to be grateful for these special people in her life and enjoy them while they're still here and enjoy God's journey and continue to put her faith in him.